Henry George

The Condition of Labor an open Letter to Pope Leo XIII

Henry George

The Condition of Labor an open Letter to Pope Leo XIII

ISBN/EAN: 9783744765015

Printed in Europe, USA, Canada, Australia, Japan

Cover: Foto ©ninafisch / pixelio.de

More available books at **www.hansebooks.com**

THE CONDITION OF LABOR

AN

OPEN LETTER TO POPE LEO XIII.

BY

HENRY GEORGE

WITH ENCYCLICAL LETTER OF POPE LEO XIII.
ON THE CONDITION OF LABOR

NEW YORK
CHARLES L. WEBSTER & COMPANY
1893

THE CONDITION OF LABOR

An Open Letter to Pope Leo XIII.

To POPE LEO XIII.

Your Holiness:

I have read with care your Encyclical letter on the condition of labor, addressed, through the Patriarchs, Primates, Archbishops and Bishops of your faith, to the Christian World.

Since its most strikingly pronounced condemnations are directed against a theory that we who hold it know to be deserving of your support, I ask permission to lay before your Holiness the grounds of our belief, and to set forth some considerations that you have unfortunately overlooked. The momentous seriousness of the facts you refer to, the poverty, suffering and seething discontent that pervade the Christian world, the danger that passion may lead ignorance in a blind struggle against social conditions rapidly becoming intolerable, are my justification.

I.

Our postulates are all stated or implied in your Encyclical. They are the primary perceptions of human reason, the fundamental teachings of the Christian faith:

We hold: That—

This world is the creation of **God**.

The men brought into it for the brief period of their earthly lives are the equal creatures of His bounty, the equal subjects of His provident care.

By his constitution man is beset by physical wants, on the satisfaction of which depend not only the maintenance of his physical life but also the development of his intellectual and spiritual life.

God has made the satisfaction of these wants dependent on man's own exertions, giving him the power and laying on him the injunction to labor—a power that of itself raises him far above the brute, since we may reverently say that it enables him to become as it were a helper in the creative work.

God has not put on man the task of making bricks without straw. With the need for labor and the power to labor He has also given to man the material for labor. This material is land—man physically being a land animal, who can live only on and from land, and can use other elements, such as air, sunshine and water, only by the use of land.

Being the equal creatures of the Creator, equally entitled under His providence to live their lives and satisfy their needs, men are equally entitled to the use of land, and any adjustment that denies this equal use of land is morally wrong.

As to the right of ownership, we hold: That—

Being created individuals, with individual wants and powers, men are individually entitled (subject of course to the moral obligations that arise from such relations as that of the family) to the use of their own powers and the enjoyment of the results.

There thus arises, anterior to human law, and deriving its validity from the law of God, a right of private ownership in things produced by labor—a right that the possessor may transfer, but of which to deprive him without his will is theft.

This right of property, originating in the right of the individual to himself, is the only full and complete right of property. It attaches to things produced by labor, but cannot attach to things created by God.

Thus, if a man take a fish from the ocean he acquires a right of property in that fish, which exclusive right he may transfer by sale or gift. But he cannot obtain a similar right of property in the ocean, so that he may sell *it* or give *it* or forbid others to use *it*.

Or, if he set up a windmill he acquires a right of property in the things such use of wind enables him to produce. But he cannot claim a right of property in the wind itself, so that he may sell *it* or forbid others to use *it*.

Or, if he cultivate grain he acquires a right of property in the grain his labor brings forth. But he cannot obtain a similar right of property in the sun which ripened it or the soil on which it grew. For these things are of the continuing gifts of God to all generations of men, which all may use, but none may claim as his alone.

To attach to things created by God the same right of private ownership that justly attaches to things produced by labor is to impair and deny the true rights of property. For a man who out of the proceeds of his labor **is obliged** to pay another man for the use of ocean **or air or sunshine or** soil, all of which are to men involved **in the** single term land, is in this **deprived of his** rightful property and thus robbed.

As to the use of land, we hold : That—
While the right of ownership that justly attaches to things produced by labor cannot attach to land, there may attach to land a right of possession. As your Holiness says, " God has not granted the earth to mankind in general in the sense that all without distinction can deal with it as they please," and regulations necessary for its best use may be fixed by human laws. But such regulations must conform to the moral law —must secure to all equal participation in the advantages of God's general bounty. The principle is the same as where a human father leaves property equally to a number of children. Some of the things thus left may be incapable of common use or of specific division. Such things may properly be assigned to some of the children, but only under condition that the equality of benefit among them all be preserved.

In the rudest social state, while industry consists in hunting, fishing, and gathering the spontaneous fruits of the earth, private possession of land is not necessary. But as men begin to cultivate the ground and expend their labor in permanent works, private possession of the land on which labor is thus expended is needed to secure the right of property in the products of labor. For who would sow if not assured of the exclusive possession needed to enable him to reap? who would attach costly works to the soil without such exclusive possession of the soil as would enable him to secure the benefit?

This right of private possession in things created by God is however very different from the right of private ownership in things produced by labor. The one is limited, the other unlimited, save in cases when the dictate of self-preservation terminates all other rights. The purpose of the one, the exclusive possession of land, is merely to secure the other, the exclusive ownership of the products of labor; and it can never rightfully be carried so far as to impair or deny this. While anyone may hold exclusive possession of land so far as it does not interfere with the equal rights of others, he can rightfully hold it no further.

Thus Cain and Abel, were there only two men on earth, might by agreement divide the earth between them. Under this compact each might claim exclusive right to his share as against the other. But neither could rightfully continue such claim against the next man born. For since no one comes into the world without God's permission, his presence attests his equal right to the use of God's bounty. For them to refuse him any use of the earth which they had divided between them would therefore be for them to commit murder. And for them to refuse him any use of the earth, unless by laboring for them or by giving them part of the products of his labor he bought it of them, would be for them to commit theft.

God's laws do not change. Though their applications may alter with altering conditions, the same principles of right and wrong that hold when men are few and industry is rude also hold amid teeming populations and complex industries. In our cities of millions and our states of scores of millions, in a civilization where the division of labor has gone so far that large numbers are hardly conscious that they are land users, it still remains true that we are all land animals and can live only on land, and that land is God's bounty to all, of which no one can be deprived without being murdered, and for which no one can be compelled to pay another without being robbed. But even in a state of society where the elaboration of industry and the increase of permanent improvements have made the need for private possession of land widespread, there is no difficulty in conforming individual possession with the equal right to land. For as soon as any piece of land will yield to the possessor a larger return than is had by similar labor on other land a value attaches to it which is shown when it is sold or rented. Thus, the value of the land itself, irrespective of the value of any improvements in or on it, always indicates the precise value of the benefit to which all are entitled in its use, as distinguished from the value which as producer or successor of a producer belongs to the possessor in individual right.

To combine the advantages of private possession with the justice of common ownership it is only necessary therefore to take for common uses what value attaches to land irrespective of any exertion of labor on it. The principle is the same as in the case referred to, where a human father leaves equally to his children things not susceptible of specific division or common use. In that case such things would be sold or rented and the value equally applied.

It is on this common sense principle that we, who term ourselves single tax men, would have the community act.

We do not propose to assert equal rights to land by keeping land common, letting any one use any part of it at any time. We do not propose the task, impossible in the present state of society, of dividing land in equal shares; still less the yet more impossible task of keeping it so divided.

We propose, leaving land in the private possession of individuals, with full liberty on their part to give, sell or bequeath it, simply to levy on it for public uses a tax that shall equal the annual value of the land itself, irrespective of the use made of it or the improvements on it. And since this would provide amply for the need of public revenues, we would accompany this tax on land values with the repeal of all taxes now levied on the products and processes of industry—which taxes, since they take from the earnings of labor, we hold to be infringements of the right of property.

This we propose, not as a cunning device of human ingenuity, but as a conforming of human regulations to the will of God.

God cannot contradict himself nor impose on his creatures laws that clash.

If it be God's command to men that they should not steal—that is to say, that they should respect the right of property which each one has in the fruits of his labor;

And if He be also the Father of all men, who in His common bounty has intended all to have equal opportunities for sharing;

Then, in any possible stage of civilization, however elaborate, there must be some way in which the exclusive right to the products of industry may be reconciled with the equal right to land.

If the Almighty be consistent with Himself, it cannot be, as say those socialists referred to by you, that in order to secure the equal participation of men in the opportunities of life and labor we must ignore the right of private property. Nor yet can it be, as you yourself in the Encyclical seem to argue, that to secure the right of private property we must ignore the equality of right in the opportunities of life and labor. To say the one thing or the other is equally to deny the harmony of God's laws.

But, the private possession of land, subject to the payment to the community of the value of any special advantage thus given to the individual, satisfies both laws, securing to all equal participation in the bounty of the Creator and to each the full ownership of the products of his labor.

Nor do we hesitate to say that this way of securing the equal right to the bounty of the Creator and the exclusive right to the products of labor is the way intended by God for raising public revenues. For we are not atheists, who deny God; nor semi-atheists, who deny that He has any concern in politics and legislation.

It is true as you say—a salutary truth too often forgotten—that "man is older than the state, and he holds the right of providing for the life of his body prior to the formation of any state." Yet, as you too perceive, it is also true that the state is in the divinely appointed order. For He who foresaw all things and provided for all things, foresaw and provided that with the increase of population and the development of industry the organization of human society into states or governments would become both expedient and necessary.

No sooner does the state arise than, as we all know, it needs revenues. This need for revenues is small at first, while population is sparse, industry rude and the functions of the state few and simple. But with growth of population and advance of civilization the functions of the state increase and larger and larger revenues are needed.

Now, He that made the world and placed man in it, He that preordained civilization as the means whereby man might rise to higher powers and become more and more conscious of the works of his Creator, must have foreseen this increasing need for state revenues and have made provision for it. That is to say: The increasing need for public revenues with social advance, being a natural, God-ordained need, there must be a right way of raising them—some way that we can truly say is the way intended by God. It is clear that this right way of raising public revenues must accord with the moral law.

Hence:

It must not take from individuals what rightfully belongs to individuals.

It must not give some an advantage over others, as by increasing the prices of what some have to sell and others must buy.

It must not lead men into temptation, by requiring

trivial oaths, by making it profitable **to lie, to swear** falsely, to bribe or to take bribes.

It must not confuse the distinctions of right and wrong, and weaken the sanctions of religion and the **state by** creating **crimes** that **are not** sins, and punish**ing men for** doing what **in itself they have an un**doubted right to do.

It must not repress industry. **It must not check commerce.** It must not punish thrift. **It must offer no** impediment to the largest production and the fairest division of wealth.

Let me ask your Holiness to consider the taxes on **the** processes **and products of** industry by which through **the civilized world** public **revenues are** collected—the **octroi duties that** surround Italian cities with barriers; the monstrous customs duties that hamper intercourse **between** so-called Christian states; **the** taxes **on occupations**, on earnings, on investments, **on the building of** houses, **on** the cultivation of fields, on **industry and thrift in all** forms. Can these **be the** ways God **has intended that** governments should raise the means they need? Have any of them the characteristics indispensable **in any plan we can deem a right one?**

All these taxes **violate the moral law. They** take **by** force what **belongs to the individual alone;** they give **to the** unscrupulous an advantage **over** the scrupulous; they **have the effect, nay are** largely intended, to increase the price of what some have **to** sell **and** others must buy; they corrupt government; **they** make oaths a mockery; they shackle commerce; **they** fine industry and **thrift;** they lessen **the wealth** that men might enjoy, and enrich some by impoverishing others.

Yet what most strikingly shows how opposed to Christianity is this system of raising public revenues is its influence on thought.

Christianity teaches us that all men are brethren; that their true interests are harmonious, not antagonistic. It gives us, as the golden rule of life, that we should do to others as we would have others do to us. But out of the system of taxing the products and processes of labor, and out of its effects in increasing the price of what some have to sell and others must buy, has grown the theory of "protection," which denies this gospel, which holds Christ ignorant of political economy and proclaims laws of national well-being utterly at variance with His teaching. This theory sanctifies national hatreds; it inculcates a universal war of hostile tariffs; it teaches peoples that their prosperity lies in imposing on the productions of other peoples restrictions they do not wish imposed on their own; and instead of the Christian doctrine of man's brotherhood it makes injury of foreigners a civic virtue.

"By their fruits you shall know them." Can anything more clearly show that to tax the products and processes of industry is not the way God intended public revenues to be raised?

But to consider what we propose—the raising of public revenues by a single tax on the value of land irrespective of improvements—is to see that in all respects this does conform to the moral law.

Let me ask your Holiness to keep in mind that the value we propose to tax, the value of land irrespective of improvements, does not come from any exertion of labor or investment of capital on or in it—the values produced in this way being values of improvement which we would exempt. The value of land irrespective of improvement is the value that attaches to land by reason of increasing population and social progress. This is a value that always goes to the owner as owner, and never does and never can go to the user; for if the user be a different person from the owner he must always pay the owner for it in rent or in purchase money; while if the user be also the owner, it is as owner, not as user, that he receives it, and by selling or renting the land he can, as owner, continue to receive it after he ceases to be a user.

Thus, taxes on land irrespective of improvement cannot lessen the rewards of industry, nor add to prices,*

---

*As to this point it may be well to add that all economists are agreed that taxes on land values irrespective of improvement or use—or what in the terminology of Political Economy is styled rent, a term distinguished from the ordinary use of the word rent by being applied solely to payments for the use of land itself—must be paid by the owner and cannot be shifted by him on the user. To explain in another way the reason given in the text Price is not determined by the will of the seller or the will of the buyer, but by the equation of demand and supply, and therefore as to things constantly demanded and constantly produced rests at a point determined by the cost of production—whatever tends to increase the cost of bringing fresh quantities of such articles to the consumer increasing price by checking supply, and whatever tends to reduce such cost decreasing price by increasing supply. Thus taxes on wheat or tobacco or cloth add to the price that the consumer must pay, and thus the cheapening in the cost of producing steel which improved processes have made in recent years has greatly reduced the price of steel. But land has no cost of production, since it is created by God, not produced by man. Its price therefore is fixed—1 (monopoly rent), where land is held in close monopoly, by what the owners can extract from the users under penalty of deprivation and consequently of starvation, and amounts to all that common labor can earn on it beyond what is necessary to life; 2 (economic rent proper), where there is no special monopoly, by what the nor in any way take from the individual what belongs to the individual. They can only take the value that attaches to land by the growth of the community, and which therefore belongs to the community as a whole.

To take land values for the state, abolishing all taxes on the products of labor, would therefore leave to the laborer the full produce of labor; to the individual all that rightfully belongs to the individual. It would impose no burden on industry, no check on commerce, no punishment on thrift; it would secure the largest production and the fairest distribution of wealth, by leaving men free to produce and to exchange as they please, without any artificial enhancement of prices; and by taking for public purposes a value that cannot be carried off, that cannot be hidden, that of all values is most easily ascertained and most certainly and

---

particular land will yield to common labor over and above what may be had by like expenditure and exertion on land having no special advantage and for which no rent is paid; and, 3 (speculative rent, which is a species of monopoly rent, telling particularly in selling price), by the expectation of future increase of value from social growth and improvement, which expectation causing land owners to withhold land at present prices has the same effect as combination.

Taxes on land values or economic rent can therefore never be shifted by the land owner to the land user, since they in no wise increase the demand for land or enable land owners to check supply by withholding land from use. Where rent depends on mere monopolization, a case I mention because rent may in this way be demanded for the use of land even before economic or natural rent arises, the taking by taxation of what the land-owners were able to extort from labor could not enable them to extort any more, since laborers, if not left enough to live on, will die. So, in the case of economic rent proper, to take from the land owners the premiums they receive, would in no way increase the superiority of their land and the demand for it. While so far as price is affected by speculative rent, to compel the land owners to pay taxes on the value of land whether they were getting any income from it or not, would make it more difficult for them to withhold land from use; and to tax the full value would not merely destroy the power but the desire to do so.

cheaply collected, it would enormously lessen the number of officials, dispense with oaths, do away with temptations to bribery and evasion, and abolish manmade crimes in themselves innocent.

But, further: That God has intended the state to obtain the revenues it needs by the taxation of land values is shown by the same order and degree of evidence that shows that God has intended the milk of the mother for the nourishment of the babe.

See how close is the analogy. In that primitive condition ere the need for the state arises there are no land values. The products of labor have value, but in the sparsity of population no value as yet attaches to land itself. But as increasing density of population and increasing elaboration of industry necessitate the organization of the state, with its need for revenues, value begins to attach to land. As population still increases and industry grows more elaborate, so the needs for public revenues increase. And at the same time and from the same causes land values increase. The connection is invariable. The value of things produced by labor tends to decline with social development, since the larger scale of production and the improvement of processes tend steadily to reduce their cost. But the value of land on which population centers goes up and up. Take Rome or Paris or London or New York or Melbourne. Consider the enormous value of land in such cities as compared with the value of land in sparsely settled parts of the same countries. To what is this due? Is it not due to the density and activity of the populations of those cities—to the very causes that require great public expenditure for streets, drains, public buildings, and all the many things needed for the health, convenience and safety of such great cities? See how with the growth of such cities the one thing that steadily increases in value is land; how the opening of roads, the building of railways, the making of any public improvement, adds to the value of land. Is it not clear that here is a natural law—that is to say a tendency willed by the Creator? Can it mean anything else than that He who ordained the state with its needs has in the values which attach to land provided the means to meet those needs?

That it does mean this and nothing else is confirmed if we look deeper still, and inquire not merely as to the intent, but as to the purpose of the intent. If we do so we may see in this natural law by which land values increase with the growth of society not only such a perfectly adapted provision for the needs of society as gratifies our intellectual perceptions by showing us the wisdom of the Creator, but a purpose with regard to the individual that gratifies our moral perceptions by opening to us a glimpse of His beneficence.

Consider: Here is a natural law by which as society advances the one thing that increases in value is land—a natural law by virtue of which all growth of population, all advance of the arts, all general improvements of whatever kind, add to a fund that both the commands of justice and the dictates of expediency prompt us to take for the common uses of society. Now, since increase in the fund available for the common uses of society is increase in the gain that goes equally to each member of society, is it not clear that the law by which land values increase with social advance while the value of the products of labor do not increase, tends with the advance of civilization to make the share that goes equally to each member of society more and more important as compared with what goes to him from his individual earnings, and thus to make the advance of civilization lessen relatively the differences that in a ruder social state must exist between the strong and the weak, the fortunate and the unfortunate? Does it not show the purpose of the Creator to be that the advance of man in civilization should be an advance not merely to larger powers but to a greater and greater equality, instead of what we, by our ignoring of His intent, are making it, an advance towards a more and more monstrous inequality?

That the value attaching to land with social growth is intended for social needs is shown by the final proof. God is indeed a jealous God in the sense that nothing but injury and disaster can attend the effort of men to do things other than in the way He has intended; in the sense that where the blessings He proffers to men are refused or misused they turn to evils that scourge us. And just as for the mother to withhold the provision that fills her breast with the birth of the child is to endanger physical health, so for society to refuse to take for social uses the provision intended for them is to breed social disease.

For refusal to take for public purposes the increasing values that attach to land with social growth is to necessitate the getting of public revenues by taxes that lessen production, distort distribution and corrupt society. It is to leave some to take what justly belongs to all; it is to forego the only means by which it is possible in an advanced civilization to combine the security of possession that is necessary to improvement with the equality of natural opportunity that is the most important of all natural rights. It is thus at the basis of all social life to set up an unjust inequality between man and man, compelling some to pay others for the privilege of living, for the chance of working, for the advantages of civilization, for the gifts of their God. But it is even more than this. The very robbery that the masses of men thus suffer gives rise in advancing communities to a new robbery. For the value that with the increase of population and social advance attaches to land being suffered to go to individuals who have secured ownership of the land, it prompts to a forestalling of and speculation in land wherever there is any prospect of advancing population or of coming improvement, thus producing an artificial scarcity of the natural elements of life and labor, and a strangulation of production that shows itself in recurring spasms of industrial depression as disastrous to the world as destructive wars. It is this that is driving men from the old countries to the new countries, only to bring there the same curses. It is this that causes our material advance not merely to fail to improve the condition of the mere worker, but to make the condition of large classes positively worse. It is this that in our richest Christian countries is giving us a large population whose lives are harder, more hopeless, more degraded than those of the veriest savages. It is this that leads so many men to think that God is a bungler and is constantly bringing more people into His world than He has made provision for; or that there is no God, and that belief in Him is a superstition which the facts of life and the advance of science are dispelling.

The darkness in light, the weakness in strength, the poverty amid wealth, the seething discontent foreboding civil strife, that characterize our civilization of to-day, are the natural, the inevitable results of our rejection of God's beneficence, of our ignoring of His intent. Were we on the other hand to follow His clear, simple rule of right, leaving scrupulously to the individual all that individual labor produces, and taking for the community the value that attaches to land by the growth of the community itself, not merely could evil modes of raising public revenues be dispensed with, but all men would be placed on an equal level of opportunity with regard to the bounty of their Creator, on an equal level of opportunity to exert their labor and to enjoy its fruits. And then, without drastic or restrictive measures the forestalling of land would cease. For then the possession of land would mean only security for the permanence of its use, and there would be no object for any one to get land or to keep land except for use; nor would his possession of better land than others had confer any unjust advantage on him, or unjust deprivation on them, since the equivalent of the advantage would be taken by the state for the benefit of all.

The Right Reverend Dr. Thomas Nulty, Bishop of Meath, who sees all this as clearly as we do, in pointing out to the clergy and laity of his diocese *

---

* Letter addressed to the Clergy and Laity of the Diocese of Meath, Ireland, April 2, 1881.

the design of Divine Providence that the rent of land should be taken for the community, says:

"I think, therefore, that I may fairly infer, on the strength of authority as well as of reason, that the people are and always must be the real owners of the land of their country. This great social fact appears to me to be of incalculable importance, and it is fortunate, indeed, that on the strictest principles of justice it is not clouded even by a shadow of uncertainty or doubt. There is, moreover, a charm and a peculiar beauty in the clearness with which it reveals the wisdom and the benevolence of the designs of Providence in the admirable provision He has made for the wants and the necessities of that state of social existence of which He is author, and in which the very instincts of nature tell us we are to spend our lives. A vast public property, a great national fund, has been placed under the dominion and at the disposal of the nation to supply itself abundantly with resources necessary to liquidate the expenses of its government, the administration of its laws and the education of its youth, and to enable it to provide for the suitable sustentation and support of its criminal and pauper population. One of the most interesting peculiarities of this property is that its value is never stationary; it is constantly progressive and increasing in a direct ratio to the growth of the population, and the very causes that increase and multiply the demands made on it increase proportionately its ability to meet them."

There is, indeed, as Bishop **Nulty** says, a peculiar beauty in the clearness with which the wisdom and benevolence of Providence are revealed in this great social fact, the provision made for the common needs of society in what economists call the law of rent. Of all the evidence that natural religion gives, it is this that most clearly shows the existence of a beneficent God, and most conclusively silences the doubts that in our days lead so many to materialism.

For in this beautiful provision made by natural law for the social needs of civilization we see that God has intended civilization; that all our discoveries and inventions do not and cannot outrun His forethought, and that steam, electricity and labor saving appliances only make the great moral laws clearer and more important. In the growth of this great fund, increasing with social advance—a fund that accrues from the growth of the community and belongs therefore to the community—we see not only that there is no need for the taxes that lessen wealth, that engender corruption, that promote inequality and teach men to deny the gospel ; but that to take this fund for the purpose for which it was evidently intended would in the highest civilization secure to all the equal enjoyment of God's bounty, the abundant opportunity to satisfy their wants, and would provide amply for every legitimate need of the state. We see that God in His dealings with men has not been a bungler or a niggard ; that He has not brought too many men into the world ; that He has not neglected abundantly to supply them; that He has not intended that bitter competition of the masses for a mere animal existence and that monstrous aggregation of wealth which characterize our civilization ; but that these evils which lead so many to say there is no God, or yet more impiously to say that they are of God's ordering, are due to our denial of His moral law. We see that the law of justice, the law of the Golden Rule, is not a mere counsel of perfection, but indeed the law of social life. We see that if we were only to observe it there would be work for all, leisure for all, abundance for all; and that civilization would tend to give to the poorest not only necessaries, but all comforts and reasonable luxuries as well. We see that Christ was not a mere dreamer when He told men that if they would seek the kingdom of God and its right doing they might no more worry about material things than do the lilies of the field about their raiment; but that He was only declaring what political economy in the light of modern discovery shows to be a sober truth.

Your Holiness, even to see this is deep and lasting joy. For it is to see for one's self that there is a God who lives and reigns, and that He is a God of justice and love—Our Father who art in Heaven. It is to open a rift of sunlight through the clouds of our darker questionings, and to make the faith that trusts where it cannot see a living thing.

II.

Your Holiness will see from the explanation I have given that the reform we propose, like all true reforms, has both an ethical and an economic side. By ignoring the ethical side, and pushing our proposal merely as a reform of taxation, we could avoid the objections that arise from confounding ownership with possession and attributing to private property in land that security of use and improvement that can be had even better without it. All that we seek practically is the legal abolition, as fast as possible, of taxes on the products and processes of labor, and the consequent concentration of taxation on land values irrespective of improvements. To put our proposals in this way would be to urge them merely as a matter of wise public expediency.

There are indeed many single tax men who do put our proposals in this way; who seeing the beauty of our plan from a fiscal standpoint do not concern themselves farther. But to those who think as I do, the ethical is the more important side. Not only do we not wish to evade the question of private property in land, but to us it seems that the beneficent and far-reaching revolution we aim at is too great a thing to be accomplished by "intelligent self-interest," and can be carried by nothing less than the religious conscience.

Hence we earnestly seek the judgment of religion. This is the tribunal of which your Holiness as the head of the largest body of Christians is the most august representative.

It therefore behooves us to examine the reasons you urge in support of private property in land—if they be sound to accept them, and if they be not sound respectfully to point out to you wherein is their error.

To your proposition that "Our first and most fundamental principle when we undertake to alleviate the condition of the masses must be the inviolability of private property" we would joyfully agree if we could only understand you to have in mind the moral element, and to mean rightful private property, as when you speak of marriage as ordained by God's authority we may understand an implied exclusion of improper marriages. Unfortunately, however, other expressions show that you mean private property in general and have expressly in mind private property in land. This confusion of thought, this non-distribation of terms, runs through your whole argument, leading you to conclusions so unwarranted by your premises as to be utterly repugnant to them, as when from the moral sanction of private property in the things produced by labor you infer something entirely different and utterly opposed, a similar right of property in the land created by God.

Private property is not of one species, and moral sanction can no more be asserted universally of it than of marriage. That proper marriage conforms to the law of God does not justify the polygamic, or polyandric or incestuous marriages that are in some countries permitted by the civil law. And as there may be immoral marriage so may there be immoral private property. Private property is that which may be held in ownership by an individual, or that which may be held in ownership by an individual with the sanction of the state. The mere lawyer, the mere servant of the state, may rest here, refusing to distinguish between what the state holds equally lawful. Your Holiness, however, is not a servant of the state, but a servant of God, a guardian of morals. You know, as said by St. Thomas of Aquin, that—

"Human law is law only in virtue of its accordance with right reason and it is thus manifest that it flows from the eternal law. And in so far as it deviates from right reason it is called an unjust law. *In such case it is not law at all, but rather a species of violence.*"

Thus, that any species of property is permitted by the state does not of itself give it moral sanction. The state has often made things property that are not justly property, but involve violence and robbery.

For instance, the things of religion, the dignity and authority of offices of the church, the power of administering her sacraments and controlling her temporalities have often by profligate princes been given as salable property to courtiers and concubines. At this very day in England an atheist or a heathen may buy in open market, and hold as legal property, to be sold, given or bequeathed as he pleases, the power of appointing to the cure of souls, and the value of these legal rights of presentation is said to be no less than £17,000,000.

Or again: Slaves were universally treated as property by the customs and laws of the classical nations, and were so acknowledged in Europe long after the acceptance of Christianity. At the beginning of this century there was no Christian nation that did not, in her colonies at least, recognize property in slaves, and slave ships crossed the seas under Christian flags. In the United States, little more than thirty years ago, to buy a man gave the same legal ownership as to buy a horse, and in Mohammedan countries law and custom yet make the slave the property of his captor or purchaser.

Yet your Holiness, one of the glories of whose pontificate is the attempt to break up slavery in its last strongholds, will not contend that the moral sanction that attaches to property in things produced by labor can, or ever could, apply to property in slaves.

Your use, in so many passages of your Encyclical, of the inclusive term " property " or " private " property, of which in morals nothing can be either affirmed or denied, makes your meaning, if we take isolated sentences, in many places ambiguous. But reading it as a whole, there can be no doubt of your intention that private property in land shall be understood when you speak merely of private property. With this interpretation, I find that the reasons you urge for private property in land are eight. Let us consider them in order of presentation. You urge:

1. *That what is bought with rightful property is rightful property.* (*5.*)*

Clearly, purchase and sale cannot give, but can only transfer ownership. Property that in itself has no moral sanction does not obtain moral sanction by passing from seller to buyer.

If right reason does not make the slave the property of the slave hunter it does not make him the property of the slave buyer. Yet your reasoning as to private property in land would as well justify property in slaves. To show this it is only needful to change in your argument the word land to the word slave. It would then read:

"It is surely undeniable that when a man engages in remunerative labor the very reason and motive of his work is to obtain property, and to hold it in his own private possession.

"If one man hire out to another his strength or his industry he does this for the purpose of receiving in return what is necessary for food and living; he thereby expressly proposes to acquire a full and legal right, not only to the remuneration, but also to the disposal of that remuneration as he pleases.

"Thus, if he lives sparingly, saves money and invests his savings for greater security in a *slave*, the *slave* in

---

* To facilitate references the paragraphs of the Encyclical are indicated by number.

such a case is only his wages in another form; and consequently a workingman's *slave* thus purchased should be as completely at his own disposal as the wages he receives for his labor."

Nor in turning your argument for private property in land into an argument for private property in men am I doing a new thing. In my own country, in my own time, this very argument, that purchase gave ownership, was the common defense of slavery. It was made by statesmen, by jurists, by clergymen, by bishops; it was accepted over the whole country by the great mass of the people. By it was justified the separation of wives from husbands, of children from parents, the compelling of labor, the appropriation of its fruits, the buying and selling of Christians by Christians. In language almost identical with yours it was asked, "Here is a poor man who has worked hard, lived sparingly, and invested his savings in a few slaves. Would you rob him of his earnings by liberating those slaves?" Or it was said: "Here is a poor widow; all her husband has been able to leave her is a few negroes, the earnings of his hard toil. Would you rob the widow and the orphan by freeing these negroes?" And because of this perversion of reason, this confounding of unjust property rights with just property rights, this acceptance of man's law as though it were God's law, there came on our nation a judgment of fire and blood.

The error of our people in thinking that what in itself was not rightfully property could become rightful property by purchase and sale is the same error into which your Holiness falls. It is not merely formally the same; it is essentially the same. Private property in land, no less than private property in slaves, is a violation of the true rights of property. They are different forms of the same robbery; twin devices by which the perverted ingenuity of man has sought to enable the strong and the cunning to escape God's requirement of labor by forcing it on others.

What difference does it make whether I merely own the land on which another man must live or own the man himself? Am I not in the one case as much his master as in the other? Can I not compel him to work for me? Can I not take to myself as much of the fruits of his labor; as fully dictate his actions? Have I not over him the power of life and death? For to deprive a man of land is as certainly to kill him as to deprive him of blood by opening his veins, or of air by tightening a halter around his neck.

The essence of slavery is in empowering one man to obtain the labor of another without recompense. Private property in land does this as fully as chattel slavery. The slave owner must leave to the slave enough of his earnings to enable him to live. Are there not in so called free countries great bodies of workingmen who get no more? How much more of the fruits of their toil do the agricultural laborers of Italy and England get than did the slaves of our Southern States? Did not private property in land permit the land owner of Europe in ruder times to demand the *jus primæ noctis?* Does not the same last outrage exist to-day in diffused form in the immorality born of monstrous wealth on the one hand and ghastly poverty on the other?

In what did the slavery of Russia consist but in giving to the master land on which the serf was forced to live? When an Ivan or a Catherine enriched their favorites with the labor of others they did not give men, they gave land. And when the appropriation of land has gone so far that no free land remains to which the landless man may turn, then without further violence the more insidious form of labor robbery involved in private property in land takes the place of chattel slavery, because more economical and convenient. For under it the slave does not have to be caught or held, or to be fed when not needed. He comes of himself, begging the privilege of serving, and when no longer wanted can be discharged. The lash is unnecessary; hunger is as efficacious. This is why the Norman conquerors of England and the English conquerors of Ireland did not divide up the people, but divided the land. This is why European slave ships took their cargoes to the New World, not to Europe.

Slavery is not yet abolished. Though in all Christian countries its ruder form has now gone, it still exists in the heart of our civilization in more insidious form, and is increasing. There is work to be done for the glory of God and the liberty of man by other soldiers of the cross than those warrior monks whom, with the blessing of your Holiness, Cardinal Lavigerie is sending into the Sahara. Yet, your Encyclical employs in defense of one form of slavery the same fallacies that the apologists for chattel slavery used in defense of the other!

The Arabs are not wanting in acumen. Your Encyclical reaches far. What shall your warrior monks say, if when at the muzzle of their rifles they demand of some Arab slave merchant his miserable caravan, he shall declare that he bought them with his savings, and producing a copy of your Encyclical, shall prove by your reasoning that his slaves are consequently "only his wages in another form," and ask if they who bear your blessing and own your authority propose to "deprive him of the liberty of disposing of his wages and thus of all hope and possibility of increasing his stock and bettering his condition in life?"

2. *That private property in land proceeds from man's gift of reason. (6–7.)*

In the second place your Holiness argues that man possessing reason and forethought may not only acquire ownership of the fruits of the earth, but also of the earth itself, so that out of its products he may make provision for the future.

Reason, with its attendant forethought, is indeed the distinguishing attribute of man; that which raises him above the brute, and shows, as the Scriptures declare, that he is created in the likeness of God. And this gift of reason does, as your Holiness points out, involve the need and right of private property in whatever is produced by the exertion of reason and its attendant forethought, as well as in what is produced by physical labor. In truth, these elements of man's production are inseparable, and labor involves the use of reason. It is by his reason that man differs from the animals in being a producer, and in this sense a maker. Of themselves his physical powers are slight, forming as it were but the connection by which the mind takes hold of material things, so as to utilize to its will the matter and forces of nature. It is mind, the intelligent reason, that is the prime mover in labor, the essential agent in production.

. The right of private ownership does therefore indisputably attach to things provided by man's reason and forethought. But it cannot attach to things provided by the reason and forethought of God!

To illustrate: Let us suppose a company travelling through the desert as the Israelites travel ed from Egypt. Such of them as had the forethought to provide themselves with vessels of water would acquire a just right of property in the water so carried, and in the thirst of the waterless desert those who had neglected to provide themselves, though they might ask water from the provident in charity, could not demand it in right. For while water itself is of the providence of God, the presence of this water in such vessels, at such place, results from the providence of the men who carried it. Thus they have to it an exclusive right.

But suppose others use their forethought in pushing ahead and appropriating the springs, refusing when their fellows come up to let them drink of the water save as they buy it of them. Would such forethought give any right?

Your Holiness, it is not the forethought of carrying water where it is needed, but the forethought of seizing springs, that you seek to defend in defending the private ownership of land!

Let me show this more fully, since it may be worth while to meet those who say that if private property in land be not just, then private property in the products of labor is not just, as the material of these products is taken from land. It will be seen on consideration that all of man's production is analogous to such transportation of water as we have supposed. In growing grain, or smelting metals, or building houses, or weaving cloth, or doing any of the things that constitute producing, all that man does is to change in place or form pre-existing matter. As a producer man is merely a changer, not a creator; God alone creates. And since the changes in which man's production consists inhere in matter so long as they persist, the right of private ownership attaches the accident to the essence, and gives the right of ownership in that natural material in which the labor of production is embodied. Thus water, which in its original form and place is the common gift of God to all men, when drawn from its natural reservoir and brought into the desert, passes rightfully into the ownership of the individual who by changing its place has produced it there.

But such right of ownership is in reality a mere right of temporary possession. For though man may take material from the storehouse of nature and change it in place or form to suit his desires, yet from the moment he takes it, it tends back to that storehouse again. Wood decays, iron rusts, stone disintegrates and is displaced, while of more perishable products, some will last for only a few months, others for only a few days, and some disappear immediately on use. Though, so far as we can see, matter is eternal and force forever persists; though we can neither annihilate nor create the tiniest mote that floats in a sunbeam or the faintest impulse that stirs a leaf, yet in the ceaseless flux of nature, man's work of moving and combining constantly passes away. Thus the recognition of the ownership of what natural material is embodied in the products of man never constitutes more than temporary possession—never interferes with the reservoir provided for all. As taking water from one place and carrying it to another place by no means lessens the store of water, since whether it is drunk or spilled or left to evaporate, it must return again to the natural reservoirs—so is it with all things on which man in production can lay the impress of his labor.

Hence, when you say that man's reason puts it within his right to have in stable and permanent possession not only things that perish in the using, but also those that remain for use in the future, you are right in so far as you may include such things as buildings, which with repair will last for generations, with such things as food or firewood, which are destroyed in the use. But when you infer that man can have private ownership in those permanent things of nature that are the reservoirs from which all must draw, you are clearly wrong. Man may indeed hold in private ownership the fruits of the earth produced by his labor, since they lose in time the impress of that labor, and pass again into the natural reservoirs from which they were taken, and thus the ownership of them by one works no injury to others. But he cannot so own the earth itself, for that is the reservoir from which must constantly be drawn not only the material with which alone men can produce, but even their very bodies.

The conclusive reason why man cannot claim ownership in the earth itself as he can in the fruits that he by labor brings forth from it, is in the facts stated by you in the very next paragraph (7), when you truly say:

"Man's needs do not die out, but recur; satisfied to-day they demand new supplies to-morrow. *Nature therefore owes to man a storehouse that shall never fail, the daily supply of his daily wants. And this he finds only in the inexhaustible fertility of the earth.*"

By man you mean all men. Can what nature owes to all men be made the private property of some men, from which they may debar all other men?

Let me dwell on the words of your Holiness, "*Nature*, therefore, *owes* to man a storehouse that shall never fail." By Nature you mean God. Thus your thought, that in creating us, God himself has incurred an obligation to provide us with a storehouse that shall never fail, is the same as is thus expressed and carried to its irresistible conclusion by the Bishop of Meath:

"God was perfectly free in the act by which He created us; but having created us He bound himself by that act to provide us with the means necessary for our subsistence. The land is the only source of this kind now known to us. The land, therefore, of every country is the common property of the people of that country, because its real owner, the Creator who made it, has transferred it as a voluntary gift to them. '*Terram autem dedit filiis hominum.*' Now, as every individual in that country is a creature and child of God, and as all His creatures are equal in His sight, any settlement of the land of a country that would exclude the humblest man in that country from his share of the common inheritance would be not only an injustice and a wrong to that man, but, moreover, be AN IMPIOUS RESISTANCE TO THE BENEVOLENT INTENTIONS OF HIS CREATOR."

· 3. *That private property in land deprives no one of the use of land.* (8.)

Your own statement that land is the inexhaustible storehouse that God owes to man must have aroused in your Holiness's mind an uneasy questioning of its appropriation as private property, for, as though to reassure yourself, you proceed to argue that its ownership by some will not injure others. You say in substance, that even though divided among private owners the earth does not cease to minister to the needs of all, since those who do not possess the soil can by selling their labor obtain in payment the produce of the land.

Suppose that to your Holiness as a judge of morals one should put this case of conscience:

"I am one of several children to whom our father left a field abundant for our support. As he assigned no part of it to any one of us in particular, leaving the limits of our separate possession to be fixed by ourselves, I being the eldest took the whole field in exclusive ownership. But in doing so I have not deprived my brothers of their support from it, for I have let them work for me on it, paying them from the produce as much wages as I would have had to pay strangers. Is there any reason why my conscience should not be clear?"

What would be your answer? Would you not tell him that he was in mortal sin, and that his excuse added to his guilt? Would you not call on him to make restitution and to do penance?

Or, suppose that as a temporal prince your Holiness were ruler of a rainless land, such as Egypt, where there were no springs or brooks, their want being supplied by a bountiful river like the Nile.

Supposing that having sent a number of your subjects to make fruitful this land, bidding them do justly and prosper, you were told that some of them had set up a claim of ownership in the river, refusing the others a drop of water, except as they bought it of them; and that thus they had become rich without work, while the others, though working hard, were so impoverished by paying for water as to be hardly able to exist?

Would not your indignation wax hot when this was told?

Suppose that then the river owners should send to you and thus excuse their action:

"The river, though divided among private owners ceases not thereby to minister to the needs of all, for there is no one who drinks who does not drink of the water of the river. Those who do not possess the water of the river contribute their labor to get it; so that it may be truly said that all water is supplied either from one's own river, or from some laborious industry which is paid for either in the water, or in that which is exchanged for the water."

Would the indignation of your Holiness be abated? Would it not wax fiercer yet for the insult to your intelligence of this excuse?

I do not need more formally to show your Holiness that between utterly depriving a man of God's gifts and depriving him of God's gifts unless he will buy them, is merely the difference between the robber who leaves his victim to die and the robber who puts him to ransom. But I would like to point out how your statement that "the earth though divided among private owners ceases not thereby to minister to the needs of all" overlooks the largest facts.

From your palace of the Vatican the eye may rest on the expanse of the Campagna, where the pious toil of religious congregations and the efforts of the state are only now beginning to make it possible for men to live. Once that expanse was tilled by thriving husbandmen and dotted with smiling hamlets. What for centuries has condemned it to desertion? History tells us. It was private property in land; the growth of the great estates of which Pliny saw that ancient Italy was perishing; the cause that, by bringing failure to the crop of men, let in the Goths and Vandals, gave Roman Britain to the worship of Odin and Thor, and in what were once the rich and populous provinces of the East shivered the thinned ranks and palsied arms of the legions on the cimiters of Mohammedan hordes, and in the sepulchre of our Lord and in the Church of St. Sophia trampled the cross to rear the crescent!

If you will go to Scotland, you may see great tracts that under the Gaelic tenure, which recognized the right of each to a foothold in the soil, bred sturdy men, but that now, under the recognition of private property in land, are given up to wild animals. If you go to Ireland, your Bishops will show you, on lands where now only beasts graze, the traces of hamlets that when they were young priests, were filled with honest, kindly, religious people.*

---

* Let any one who wishes visit this diocese and see with his own eyes the vast and boundless extent of the fairest land in Europe that has been ruthlessly depopulated since the commencement of the present century, and which is now abandoned to a loneliness and solitude more depressing than that of the prairie or the wilderness. Thus has this land system actually exercised the power of life and death on a vast scale, for which there is no parallel even in the dark records of slavery. —*Bishop Nulty's letter to the Clergy and Laity of the Diocese of Meath.*

If you will come to the United States, you will find in a land wide enough and rich enough to support in comfort the whole population of Europe, the growth of a sentiment that looks with evil eye on immigration, because the artificial scarcity that results from private property in land makes it seem as if there is not room enough and work enough for those already here.

Or go to the Antipodes, and in Australia as in England, you may see that private property in land is operating to leave the land barren and to crowd the bulk of the population into great cities. Go wherever you please where the forces loosed by modern invention are beginning to be felt and you may see that private property in land is the curse, denounced by the prophet, that prompts men to lay field to field till they "alone dwell in the midst of the earth."

To the mere materialist this is sin and shame. Shall we to whom this world is God's world—we who hold that man is called to this life only as a prelude to a higher life—shall we defend it?

4. *That Industry expended on land gives ownership in the land itself.* (9–10.)

Your Holiness next contends that industry expended on land gives a right to ownership of the land, and that the improvement of land creates benefits indistinguishable and inseparable from the land itself.

This contention, if valid, could only justify the ownership of land by those who expend industry on it. It would not justify private property in land as it exists. On the contrary, it would justify a gigantic no-rent declaration that would take land from those who now legally own it, the landlords, and turn it over to the tenants and laborers. And if it also be that improvements cannot be distinguished and separated from the land itself, how could the landlords claim consideration even for improvements they had made?

But your Holiness cannot mean what your words imply. What you really mean, I take it, is that the original justification and title of land ownership is in the expenditure of labor on it. But neither can this justify private property in land as it exists. For is it not all but universally true that existing land titles do not come from use, but from force or fraud?

Take Italy! Is it not true that the greater part of the land of Italy is held by those who so far from ever having expended industry on it have been mere appropriators of the industry of those who have? Is this not also true of Great Britain and of other countries? Even in the United States, where the forces of concentration have not yet had time to fully operate and there has been some attempt to give land to users, it is probably true to-day that the greater part of the land is held by those who neither use it nor propose to use it themselves, but merely hold it to compel others to pay them for permission to use it.

And if industry give ownership to land what are the limits of this ownership? If a man may acquire the ownership of several square miles of land by grazing sheep on it, does this give to him and his heirs the ownership of the same land when it is found to contain rich mines, or when by the growth of population and the progress of society it is needed for farming, for gardening, for the close occupation of a great city? Is it on the rights given by the industry of those who first used it for grazing cows or growing potatoes that you would found the title to the land now covered by the city of New York and having a value of thousands of millions of dollars?

But your contention is not valid. Industry expended on land gives ownership in the fruits of that industry, but not in the land itself, just as industry expended on the ocean would give a right of ownership to the fish taken by it, but not a right of ownership in the ocean. Nor yet is it true that private ownership of land is necessary to secure the fruits of labor on land; nor does the improvement of land create benefits indistinguishable and inseparable from the land itself. That secure possession is necessary to the use and improvement of land I have already explained, but that ownership is not necessary is shown by the fact that in all civilized countries land owned by one person is cultivated and improved by other persons. Most of the cultivated land in the British Islands, as in Italy and other countries, is cultivated not by owners but by tenants. And so the costliest buildings are erected by those who are not owners of the land, but who have from the owner a mere right of possession for a time on condition of certain payments. Nearly the whole of London has been built in this way, and in New York, Chicago, Denver, San Francisco, Sydney and Melbourne, as well as in continental cities, the owners of many of the largest edifices will be found to be different persons from the owners of the ground. So far from the value of improvements being inseparable from the value of land, it is in individual transactions constantly separated. For instance, one-half of the land on which the immense Grand Pacific Hotel in Chicago stands was recently separately sold, and in Ceylon it is a not infrequent occurrence for one person to own a fruit tree and another to own the ground in which it is implanted.

There is, indeed, no improvement of land, whether it be clearing, plowing, manuring, cultivating, the digging of cellars, the opening of wells or the building of houses, that so long as its usefulness continues does not have a value clearly distinguishable from the value of the land. For land having such improvements will always sell or rent for more than similar land without them.

If, therefore, the state levy a tax equal to what the land irrespective of improvement would bring, it will take the benefits of mere ownership, but will leave the full benefits of use and improvement, which the prevailing system does not do. And since the holder, who would still in form continue to be the owner, could at any time give or sell both possession and improvements, subject to future assessment by the state on the value of the land alone, he will be perfectly free to retain or dispose of the full amount of property that the exertion of his labor or the investment of his capital has attached to or stored up in the land.

Thus, what we propose would secure, as it is impossible in any other way to secure, what you properly say is just and right—"that the results of labor should belong to him who has labored." But private property in land—to allow the holder without adequate payment to the state to take for himself the benefit of the value that attaches to land with social growth and improvement—does take the results of labor from him who has labored, does turn over the fruits of one man's labor to be enjoyed by another. For labor, as the active factor, is the producer of all wealth. Mere ownership produces nothing. A man might own a world, but so sure is the decree that "by the sweat of thy brow shalt thou eat bread," that without labor he could not get a meal or provide himself a garment. Hence, when the owners of land, by virtue of their ownership and without laboring themselves, get the products of labor in abundance, these things must come from the labor of others, must be the fruits of others' sweat, taken from those who have a right to them and enjoyed by those who have no right to them.

The only utility of private ownership of land as distinguished from possession is the evil utility of giving to the owner products of labor he does not earn. For until land will yield to its owner some return beyond that of the labor and capital he expends on it—that is to say, until by sale or rental he can without expenditure of labor obtain from it products of labor, ownership amounts to no more than security of possession, and has no value. Its importance and value begin only when, either in the present or prospectively, it will yield a revenue—that is to say, will enable the owner as owner to obtain products of labor without exertion on his part, and thus to enjoy the results of others' labor.

What largely keeps men from realizing the robbery involved in private property in land is that in the most striking cases the robbery is not of individuals, but of the community. For, as I have before explained, it is impossible for rent in the economic sense—that value which attaches to land by reason of social growth and improvement—to go to the user. It can go only to the owner or to the community. Thus those who pay enormous rents for the use of land in such centres as London or New York are not individually injured. Individually they get a return for what they pay, and must feel that they have no better right to the use of such peculiarly advantageous localities without paying for it than have thousands of others. And so, not thinking or not caring for the interests of the community, they make no objection to the system.

It recently came to light in New York that a man having no title whatever had been for years collecting rents on a piece of land that the growth of the city had made very valuable. Those who paid these rents had never stopped to ask whether he had any right to them. They felt that they had no right to land that so many others would like to have, without paying for it, and did not think of, or did not care for, the rights of all.

5. *That private property in land has the support of the common opinion of mankind, and has conduced to peace and tranquility, and that it is sanctioned by Divine Law.* (*11.*)

Even were it true that the common opinion of mankind has sanctioned private property in land, this would no more prove its justice than the once universal practice of the known world would have proved the justice of slavery.

But it is not true. Examination will show that wherever we can trace them the first perceptions of mankind have always recognized the equality of right to land, and that when individual possession became necessary to secure the right of ownership in things produced by labor some method of securing equality, sufficient in the existing state of social development, was adopted. Thus, among some peoples, land used for cultivation was periodically divided, land used for pasturage and wood being held in common. Among others, every family was permitted to hold what land it needed for a dwelling and for cultivation, but the moment that such use and cultivation stopped any one else could step in and take it on like tenure. Of the same nature were the land laws of the Mosaic code. The land, first fairly divided among the people, was made inalienable by the provision of the jubilee, under which, if sold, it reverted every fiftieth year to the children of its original possessors.

Private property in land as we know it, the attaching to land of the same right of ownership that justly attaches to the products of labor, has never grown up anywhere save by usurpation or force. Like slavery, it is the result of war. It comes to us of the modern world from your ancestors, the Romans, whose civilization it corrupted and whose empire it destroyed.

It made with the freer spirit of the northern peoples the combination of the feudal system, in which, though subordination was substituted for equality, there was still a rough recognition of the principle of common rights in land. A fief was a trust, and to enjoyment was annexed some obligation. The sovereign, the representative of the whole people, was the only owner of land. Of him, immediately or mediately, held tenants, whose possession involved duties or payments, which, though rudely and imperfectly, embodied the idea that we would carry out in the single tax, of taking land values for public uses. The crown lands maintained the sovereign and the civil list; the church lands defrayed the cost of public worship and instruction, of the relief of the sick, the destitute and the wayworn; while the military tenures provided for public defense and bore the costs of war. A fourth and very large portion of the land remained in common, the people of the neighborhood being free to pasture it, cut wood on it, or put it to other common uses.

In this partial yet substantial recognition of common rights to land is to be found the reason why, in a time when the industrial arts were rude, wars frequent, and the great discoveries and inventions of our time unthought of, the condition of the laborer was devoid of that grinding poverty which despite our marvellous advances now exists. Speaking of England, the highest authority on such subjects, the late Professor Thorold Rogers, declares that in the thirteenth century there was no class so poor, so helpless, so pressed and degraded as are millions of Englishmen in our boasted nineteenth century; and that, save in times of actual famine, there was no laborer so poor as to fear that his wife and children might come to want even were he taken from them. Dark and rude in many respects as they were, these were the times when the cathedrals and churches and religious houses whose ruins yet excite our admiration were built; the times when England had no national debt, no poor law, no standing army, no hereditary paupers, no thousands and thousands of human beings rising in the morning without knowing where they might lay their heads at night.

With the decay of the feudal system, the system of private property in land that had destroyed Rome was extended. As to England, it may briefly be said that the crown lands were for the most part given away to favorites; that the church lands were parcelled among his courtiers by Henry VIII., and in Scotland grasped by the nobles; that the military dues were finally remitted in the seventeenth century, and taxation on consumption substituted; and that by a process beginning with the Tudors and extending to our own time all but a mere fraction of the commons were enclosed by the greater land owners; while the same private ownership of land was extended over Ireland and the Scottish Highlands, partly by the sword and partly by bribery of the chiefs. Even the military dues, had they been commuted, not remitted, would to-day have more than sufficed to pay all public expenses without one penny of other taxation.

Of the New World, whose institutions but continue those of Europe, it is only necessary to say that to the parcelling out of land in great tracts is due the backwardness and turbulence of Spanish America; that to the large plantations of the Southern States of the Union was due the persistence of slavery there, and that the more northern settlements showed the earlier English feeling, land being fairly well divided and the attempts to establish manorial estates coming to little or nothing. In this lies the secret of the more vigorous growth of the northern states. But the idea that land was to be treated as private property had been thoroughly established in English thought before the colonial period ended, and it has been so treated by the United States and by the several States. And though land was at first sold cheaply, and then given to actual settlers, it was also sold in large quantities to speculators, given away in great tracts for railroads and other purposes, until now the public domain of the United States, which a generation ago seemed illimitable, has practically gone. And this, as the experience of other countries shows, is the natural result in a growing community of making land private property. When the possession of land means the gain of unearned wealth, the strong and unscrupulous will secure it. But when, as we propose, economic rent, the "unearned increment of wealth," is taken by the state for the use of the community, then land will pass into the hands of users and remain there, since no matter how great its value, its possession will only be profitable to users.

As to private property in land having conduced to the peace and tranquility of human life, it is not necessary more than to allude to the notorious fact that the struggle for land has been the prolific source of wars and of law suits, while it is the poverty engendered by private property in land that make the prison and the workhouse the unfailing attributes of what we call Christian civilization.

Your Holiness intimates that the Divine Law gives its sanction to the private ownership of land, quoting from Deuteronomy, "Thou shalt not covet thy neighbor's wife, nor his house, nor his field, nor his manservant, nor his maid-servant, nor his ox, nor his ass, nor anything which is his."

If, as your Holiness conveys, this inclusion of the words, "nor his field," is to be taken as sanctioning private property in land as it exists to-day, then, but with far greater force, must the words, "his manservant, nor his maid-servant," be taken to sanction chattel slavery; for it is evident from other provisions of the same code that these terms referred both to bondsmen for a term of years and to perpetual slaves. But the word "field" involves the idea of use and improvement, to which the right of possession and ownership does attach without recognition of property in the land itself. And that this reference to the "field" is not a sanction of private property in land as it exists to-day is proved by the fact that the Mosaic code expressly denied such unqualified ownership in land, and with the declaration, "the land also shall not be sold forever, because it is mine, and you are strangers and sojourners with me," provided for its reversion every fiftieth year; thus, in a way adapted to the primitive industrial conditions of the time, securing to all of the chosen people a foothold in the soil.

Nowhere in fact throughout the Scriptures can the slightest justification be found for the attaching to land of the same right of property that justly attaches to the things produced by labor. Everywhere is it treated as the free bounty of God, "the land which the Lord thy God giveth thee."

6. *That fathers should provide for their children and that private property in land is necessary to enable them to do so. (14–17.)*

With all that your Holiness has to say of the sacredness of the family relation we are in full accord. But how the obligation of the father to the child can justify private property in land we cannot see. You reason that private property in land is necessary to the discharge of the duty of the father, and is therefore requisite and just, because—

"It is a most sacred law of nature that a father must provide food and all necessities for those whom he has begotten; and similarly nature dictates that a man's children, who carry on as it were and continue his own personality, should be provided by him with all that is needful to enable them honorably to keep themselves from want and misery in the uncertainties of this mortal life. Now in no other way can a father effect this except by the ownership of profitable property, which he can transmit to his children by inheritance." (14.)

Thanks to Him who has bound the generations of men together by a provision that brings the tenderest love to greet our entrance into the world and soothes our exit with filial piety, it is both the duty and the joy of the father to care for the child till its powers mature, and afterwards in the natural order it becomes the duty and privilege of the child to be the stay of the parent. This is the natural reason for that relation of marriage, the ground work of the sweetest, tenderest and purest of human joys, which the Catholic Church has guarded with such unremitting vigilance.

We do, for a few years, need the providence of our fathers after the flesh. But how small, how transient, how narrow is this need, as compared with our constant need for the providence of Him in whom we live, move and have our being—Our Father who art in Heaven! It is to Him, "the giver of every good and perfect gift," and not to our fathers after the flesh, that Christ taught us to pray, "Give us this day our daily bread." And how true it is that it is through

Him that the generations of men exist. Let the mean temperature of the earth rise or fall a few degrees, an amount as nothing compared with differences produced in our laboratories, and mankind would disappear as ice disappears under a tropical sun, would fall as the leaves fall at the touch of frost. Or, let for two or three seasons the earth refuse her increase, and how many of our millions would remain alive?

The duty of fathers to transmit to their children profitable property that will enable them to keep themselves from want and misery in the uncertainties of this mortal life! What is not possible cannot be a duty. And how is it possible for fathers to do that? Your Holiness has not considered how mankind really lives from hand to mouth, getting each day its daily bread; how little one generation does or can leave another. It is doubtful if the wealth of the civilized world all told amounts to anything like as much as one year's labor, while it is certain that if labor were to stop and men had to rely on existing accumulation, it would be only a few days ere in the richest countries pestilence and famine would stalk.

The profitable property your Holiness refers to, is private property in land. Now profitable land, as all economists will agree, is land superior to the land that the ordinary man can get. It is land that will yield an income to the owner as owner, and therefore that will permit the owner to appropriate the products of labor without doing labor, its profitableness to the individual involving the robbery of other individuals. It is therefore possible only for some fathers to leave their children profitable land. What therefore your Holiness practically declares is, that it is the duty of all fathers to struggle to leave their children what only the few peculiarly strong, lucky or unscrupulous can leave; and that, a something that involves the robbery of others—their deprivation of the material gifts of God.

This anti-Christian doctrine has been long in practice throughout the Christian world. What are its results?

Are they not the very evils set forth in your Encyclical? Are they not, so far from enabling men to keep themselves from want and misery in the uncertainties of this mortal life, to condemn the great masses of men to want and misery that the natural conditions of our mortal life do not entail; to want and misery deeper and more widespread than exist among heathen savages? Under the regime of private property in land and in the richest countries not five per cent. of fathers are able at their death to leave anything substantial to their children, and probably a large majority do not leave enough to bury them! Some few children are left by their fathers richer than it is good for them to be, but the vast majority not only are left nothing by their fathers, but by the system that makes land private property are deprived of the bounty of their Heavenly Father; are compelled to sue others for permission to live and to work, and to toil all their lives for a pittance that often does not enable them to escape starvation and pauperism.

What your Holiness is actually, though of course inadvertently, urging, is that earthly fathers should assume the functions of the Heavenly Father. It is not the business of one generation to provide the succeeding generation with "all that is needful to enable them honorably to keep themselves from want and misery." That is God's business. We no more create our children than we create our fathers. It is God who is the Creator of each succeeding generation as fully as of the one that preceded it. And, to recall your own words (7), "Nature [God] therefore owes to man a storehouse that shall never fail, the daily supply of his daily wants. And this he finds only in the inexhaustible fertility of the earth." What you are now assuming is, that it is the duty of men to provide for the wants of *their* children by appropriating this storehouse and depriving other men's children of the unfailing supply that God has provided for all.

The duty of the father to the child—the duty possible to all fathers! Is it not so to conduct himself, so to nurture and teach it, that it shall come to manhood with a sound body, well developed mind, habits of virtue, piety and industry, and in a state of society that shall give it and all others free access to the bounty of God, the providence of the All-Father?

In doing this the father would be doing more to secure his children from want and misery than is possible now to the richest of fathers—as much more as the providence of God surpasses that of man. For the justice of God laughs at the efforts of men to circumvent it, and the subtle law that binds humanity together poisons the rich in the sufferings of the poor. Even the few who are able in the general struggle to leave their children wealth that they fondly think will keep them from want and misery in the uncertainties of this mortal life—do they succeed? Does experience show that it is a benefit to a child to place him above his fellows and enable him to think God's law of labor is not for him? Is not such wealth oftener a curse than a blessing, and does not its expectation often destroy filial love and bring dissensions and heart burnings into families? And how far and how long are even the richest and strongest able to exempt their children from the common lot? Nothing is more certain than that the blood of the masters of the world flows to-day in lazzaroni and that the descendants of kings and princes tenant slums and workhouses.

But in the state of society we strive for, where the monopoly and waste of God's bounty would be done away with and the fruits of labor would go to the laborer, it would be within the ability of all to make more than a comfortable living with reasonable labor. And for those who might be crippled or incapacitated, or deprived of their natural protectors and bread winners, the most ample provision could be made out of that great and increasing fund with which God in his law of rent has provided society—not as a matter of niggardly and degrading alms, but as a matter of right, as the assurance which in a Christian state society owes to all its members.

Thus it is that the duty of the father, the obligation to the child, instead of giving any support to private property in land, utterly condemns it, urging us by the most powerful considerations to abolish it in the simple and efficacious way of the single tax.

This duty of the father, this obligation to children, is not confined to those who have actually children of their own, but rests on all of us who have come to the powers and responsibilities of manhood.

For did not Christ set a little child in the midst of the disciples, saying to them that the angels of such little ones always behold the face of His father; saying to them that it were better for a man to hang a millstone about his neck and plunge into the uttermost depths of the sea than to injure such a little one?

And what to-day is the result of private property in land in the richest of so called Christian countries? Is it not that young people fear to marry; that married people fear to have children; that children are driven out of life from sheer want of proper nourishment and care, or compelled to toil when they ought to be at school or at play; that great numbers of those who attain maturity enter it with under-nourished bodies, overstrained nerves, undeveloped minds— under conditions that foredoom them, not merely to suffering, but to crime; that fit them in advance for the prison and the brothel?

If your Holiness will consider these things we are confident that instead of defending private property in land you will condemn it with anathema!

7. *That the private ownership of land stimulates industry, increases wealth, and attaches men to the soil and to their country.* (*51.*)

The idea, as expressed by Arthur Young, that "the magic of property turns barren sands to gold" springs from the confusion of ownership with possession, of which I have before spoken, that attributes to private property in land what is due to security of the products of labor. It is needless for me again to point out that the change we propose, the taxation for public uses of land values, or economic rent, and the abolition of other taxes, would give to the user of land far greater security for the fruits of his labor than the present system and far greater permanence of possession. Nor is it necessary further to show how it would give homes to those who are now homeless and bind men to their country. For under it every one who wanted a piece of land for a home or for productive use could get it without purchase price and hold it even without tax, since the tax we propose would not fall on all land, nor even on all land in use, but only on land better than the poorest land in use, and is in reality not a tax at all, but merely a return to the state for the use of a valuable privilege. And even those who from circumstances or occupation did not wish to make permanent use of land would still have an equal interest with all others in the land of their country and in the general prosperity.

But I should like your Holiness to consider how utterly unnatural is the condition of the masses in the richest and most progressive of Christian countries; how large bodies of them live in habitations in which a rich man would not ask his dog to dwell; how the great majority have no homes from which they are not liable on the slightest misfortune to be evicted; how numbers have no homes at all, but must seek what shelter chance or charity offers. I should like to ask your Holiness to consider how the great majority of men in such countries have no interest whatever in what they are taught to call *their* native land, for which they are told that on occasions it is their duty to fight or to die. What right, for instance, have the majority of your countrymen in the land of their birth? Can they live in Italy outside of a prison or a poorhouse except as they buy the privilege from some of the exclusive owners of Italy? Cannot an Englishman, an American, an Arab or a Japanese do as much? May not what was said centuries ago by Tiberius Gracchus be said to-day: "*Men of Rome! you are called the lords of the world, yet have no right to a square foot of its soil! The wild beasts have their dens, but the soldiers of Italy have only water and air!*"

What is true of Italy is true of the civilized world—is becoming increasingly true. It is **the inevitable effect as civilization progresses** of **private property in land.**

8. *That the right to possess private property in land* **is from** *Nature, not from man; that the state* **has no right to** *abolish it, and that to take the value of land* **ownership** *in taxation would be unjust and cruel to the private* **owner. (51).**

This, like **much else** that your Holiness says, **is masked in the use of the** indefinite terms **private** property **and private** owner—a want of precision in the use **of words that** has doubtless aided in the confusion of your own thought. But the context leaves no doubt that by private property you mean private property in land, and by private owner, the private owner of land.

The contention, thus made, that private property in land is from nature, not from man, has no other basis than the confounding of ownership with possession and the ascription to property in land of what belongs to its contradictory, property in the proceeds of labor. You do not attempt to show for it any other basis, nor has any one else ever attempted to do so. That private property in the products of labor is from nature is clear, for nature gives such things to labor and to labor alone. Of every article of this kind, we know that it came into being as nature's response to the exertion of an individual man or of individual men—given by nature directly and exclusively to him or to them. Thus there inheres in such things a right of private property, which originates from and goes back to the source of ownership, the maker of the thing. This right is anterior to the state and superior to its enactments, so that, as we hold, it is a violation of natural right and an injustice to the private owner for the state to tax the processes and products of labor. They do not belong to Cæsar. They are things that God, of whom nature is but an expression, gives to those who apply for them in the way He has appointed—by labor.

But who will dare trace the individual ownership of land to any grant from the Maker of land? What does nature give to such ownership? how does she in any way recognize it? Will any one show from difference of form or feature, of stature or complexion, from dissection of their bodies or analysis of their powers and needs, that one man was intended by nature to own land and another to live on it as his tenant? That which derives its existence from man and passes away like him, which is indeed but the evanescent expression of his labor, man may hold and transfer as the exclusive property of the individual; but how can such individual ownership attach to land, which existed before man was, and which continues to exist while the generations of men come and go—the unfailing storehouse that the Creator gives to man for "the daily supply of his daily wants?"

Clearly, the private ownership of land is from the

state, not from nature. Thus, not merely can no objection be made on the score of morals when it is proposed that the state shall abolish it altogether, but insomuch as it is a violation of natural right, its existence involving a gross injustice on the part of the state, an "impious violation of the benevolent intention of the Creator," it is a moral duty that the state so abolish it.

So far from there being anything unjust in taking the full value of land ownership for the use of the community, the real injustice is in leaving it in private hands—an injustice that amounts to robbery and murder.

And when your Holiness shall see this I have no fear that you will listen for one moment to the impudent plea that before the community can take what God intended it to take, before men who have been disinherited of their natural rights can be restored to them, the present owners of land shall first be compensated.

For not only will you see that the single tax will directly and largely benefit small land owners, whose interests as laborers and capitalists are much greater than their interests as land owners, and that though the great landowners—or rather the propertied class in general among whom the profits of land ownership are really divided through mortgages, rent charges, etc.—would relatively lose, they too would be absolute gainers in the increased prosperity and improved morals; but more quickly, more strongly, more peremptorily than from any calculation of gains or losses would your duty as a man, your faith as a Christian. forbid you to listen for one moment to any such paltering with right and wrong.

Where the state takes some land for public uses it is only just that those whose land is taken should be compensated, otherwise some land owners would be treated more harshly than others. But where, by a measure affecting all alike, rent is appropriated for the benefit of all, there can be no claim to compensation. Compensation in such case would be a continuance of the same injustice in another form—the giving to land owners in the shape of interest of what they before got as rent. Your Holiness knows that justice and injustice are not thus to be juggled with, and when you fully realize that land is really the storehouse that God owes to all His children, you will no more listen to any demand for compensation for restoring it to them than Moses would have listened to a demand that Pharaoh should be compensated before letting the children of Israel go.

Compensated for what? For giving up what has been unjustly taken? The demand of land owners for compensation is not that. We do not seek to spoil the Egyptians. We do not ask that what has been unjustly taken from laborers shall be restored. We are willing that bygones should be bygones and to leave dead wrongs to bury their dead. We propose to let those who by the past appropriation of land value have taken the fruits of labor to retain what they have thus got. We merely propose that for the future such robbery of labor shall cease—that for the future, not for the past, landholders shall pay to the community the rent that to the community is justly due.

III.

I have said enough to show your Holiness the injustice into which you fall in classing us, who in seeking virtually to abolish private property in land seek more fully to secure the true rights of property, with those whom you speak of as socialists, who wish to make all property common. But you also do injustice to the socialists.

There are many, it is true, who feeling bitterly the monstrous wrongs of the present distribution of wealth are animated only by a blind hatred of the rich and a fierce desire to destroy existing social adjustments. This class is indeed only less dangerous than those who proclaim that no social improvement is needed or is possible. But it is not fair to confound with them those who, however mistakenly, propose definite schemes of remedy.

The socialists, as I understand them, and as the term has come to apply to anything like a definite theory and not to be vaguely and improperly used to include all who desire social improvement, do not, as you imply, seek the abolition of all private property. Those who do this are properly called communists. What the socialists seek is the state assumption of capital (in which they vaguely and erroneously include land), or more properly speaking, of large capitals, and state management and direction of at least the larger operations of industry. In this way they hope to abolish interest, which they regard as a wrong and an evil; to do away with the gains of exchangers, speculators, contractors and middlemen, which they regard as waste; to do away with the wage system and secure general co-operation; and to prevent competition, which they deem the fundamental cause of the impoverishment of labor. The more moderate of them, without going so far, go in the same direction, and seek some remedy or palliation of the worst forms of poverty by government regulation. The essential character of socialism is that it looks to the extension of the functions of the state for the remedy of social evils; that it would substitute regulation and direction for competition; and intelligent control by organized society for the free play of individual desire and effort.

Though not usually classed as socialists, both the trades unionists and the protectionists have the same essential character. The trades unionists seek the increase of wages, the reduction of working hours and the general improvement in the condition of wage-workers, by organizing them into guilds or associations which shall fix the rates at which they will sell their labor; shall deal as one body with employers in case of dispute; shall use on occasion their necessary weapon, the strike; and shall accumulate funds for such purposes and for the purpose of assisting members when on a strike, or (sometimes) when out of employment. The protectionists seek by governmental prohibitions or taxes on imports to regulate the industry and control the exchanges of each country, so, as they imagine, to diversify home industries and prevent the competition of people of other countries.

At the opposite extreme are the anarchists, a term which, though frequently applied to mere violent destructionists, refers also to those who, seeing the many evils of too much government, regard government in itself as evil, and believe that in the absence of coercive power the mutual interests of men would secure voluntarily what co-operation is needed.

Differing from all these are those for whom I would speak. Believing that the rights of true property are sacred, we would regard forcible communism as robbery that would bring destruction. But we would not be disposed to deny that voluntary communism might be the highest possible state of which men can conceive. Nor do we say that it cannot be possible for mankind to attain it, since among the early Christians and among the religious orders of the Catholic church we have examples of communistic societies on a small scale. St. Peter and St. Paul, St. Thomas of Aquin and Fra Angelico, the illustrious orders of the Carmelites and Franciscans, the Jesuits, whose heroism carried the cross among the most savage tribes of American forests, the societies that wherever your communion is known have deemed no work of mercy too dangerous or too repellent—were or are communists. Knowing these things we cannot take it on ourselves to say that a social condition may not be possible in which an all-embracing love shall have taken the place of all other motives. But we see that communism is only possible where there exists a general and intense religious faith, and we see that such a state can be reached only through a state of justice. For before a man can be a saint he must first be an honest man.

With both anarchists and socialists, we, who for want of a better term have come to call ourselves single tax men, fundamentally differ. We regard them as erring in opposite directions—the one in ignoring the social nature of man, the other in ignoring his individual nature. While we see that man is primarily an individual, and that nothing but evil has come or can come from the interference by the state with things that belong to individual action, we also see that he is a social being, or, as Aristotle called him, a political animal, and that the state is requisite to social advance, having an indispensable place in the natural order. Looking on the bodily organism as the analogue of the social organism, and on the proper functions of the state as akin to those that in the human organism are discharged by the conscious intelligence, while the play of individual impulse and interest performs functions akin to those discharged in the bodily organism by the unconscious instincts and involuntary motions, the anarchists seem to us like men who would try to get along without heads and the socialists like men who would try to rule the wonderfully complex and delicate internal relations of their frames by conscious will.

The philosophical anarchists of whom I speak are few in number, and of little practical importance. It is with socialism in its various phases that we have to do battle.

With the socialists we have some points of agreement, for we recognize fully the social nature of man and believe that all monopolies should be held and governed by the state. In these, and in directions where the general health, knowledge, comfort and convenience might be improved, we, too, would extend the functions of the state.

But it seems to us the vice of socialism in all its degrees is its want of radicalism, of going to the root. It takes its theories from those who have sought to justify the impoverishment of the masses, and its advocates generally teach the preposterous and degrading doctrine that slavery was the first condition of labor. It assumes that the tendency of wages to a minimum is the natural law, and seeks to abolish wages; it assumes that the natural result of competition is to grind down workers, and seeks to abolish competition by restrictions, prohibitions and extensions of governing power. Thus mistaking effects for causes, and childishly blaming the stone for hitting it, it wastes strength in striving for remedies that when not worse are futile. Associated though it is in many places with democratic aspiration, yet its essence is the same delusion to which the Children of Israel yielded when against the protest of their prophet they insisted on a king; the delusion that has everywhere corrupted democracies and enthroned tyrants—that power over the people can be used for the benefit of the people; that there may be devised machinery that through human agencies will secure for the management of individual affairs more wisdom and more virtue than the people themselves possess.

This superficiality and this tendency may be seen in all the phases of socialism.

Take, for instance, protectionism. What support it has, beyond the mere selfish desire of sellers to compel buyers to pay them more than their goods are worth, springs from such superficial ideas as that production, not consumption, is the end of effort; that money is more valuable than money's worth, and to sell more profitable than to buy; and above all from a desire to limit competition, springing from an unanalyzing recognition of the phenomena that necessarily follow when men who have the need to labor are deprived by monopoly of access to the natural and indispensable element of all labor. Its methods involve the idea that governments can more wisely direct the expenditure of labor and the investment of capital than can laborers and capitalists, and that the men who control governments will use this power for the general good and not in their own interests. They tend to multiply officials, restrict liberty, invent crimes. They promote perjury, fraud and corruption. And they would, were the theory carried to its logical conclusion, destroy civilization and reduce mankind to savagery.

Take trades unionism. While within narrow lines trades unionism promotes the idea of the mutuality of interests, and often helps to raise courage and further political education, and while it has enabled limited bodies of workingmen to improve somewhat their condition, and gain, as it were, breathing space, yet it takes no note of the general causes that determine the conditions of labor, and strives for the elevation of only a small part of the great body by means that cannot help the rest. Aiming at the restriction of competition—the limitation of the right to labor, its methods are like those of an army, which even in a righteous cause are subversive of liberty and liable to abuse, while its weapon, the strike, is destructive in its nature, both to combatants and non-combatants, being a form of passive war. To apply the principle of trades unions to all industry, as some dream of doing, would be to enthrall men in a caste system.

Or take even such moderate measures as the limitation of working hours and of the labor of women and children. They are superficial in looking no further than to the eagerness of men and women and little children to work unduly, and in proposing forcibly to restrain overwork while utterly ignoring its cause, the sting of poverty that forces human beings to it. And the methods by which these restraints must be enforced, multiply officials, interfere with personal liberty, tend to corruption, and are liable to abuse.

As for thorough going socialism, which is the more to be honored as having the courage of its convictions, it would carry these vices to full expression. Jumping to conclusions without effort to discover causes, it fails to see that oppression does not come from the nature of capital, but from the wrong that robs labor of capital by divorcing it from land, and that creates a fictitious capital that is really capitalized monopoly. It fails to see that it would be impossible for capital to oppress labor were labor free to the natural material of production; that the wage system in itself springs from mutual convenience, being a form of co-operation in which one of the parties prefers a certain to a contingent result; and that what it calls the "iron law of wages" is not the natural law of wages, but only the law of wages in that unnatural condition in which men are made helpless by being deprived of the materials for life and work. It fails to see that what it mistakes for the evils of competition are really the evils of restricted competition— are due to a one sided competition to which men are forced when deprived of land. While its methods, the organization of men into industrial armies, the direction and control of all production and exchange by governmental or semi-governmental bureaus, would, if carried to full expression, mean Egyptian despotism.

We differ from the socialists in our diagnosis of the evil and we differ from them as to remedies. We have no fear of capital, regarding it as the natural handmaiden of labor; we look on interest in itself as natural and just; we would set no limit to accumulation, nor impose on the rich any burden that is not equally placed on the poor; we see no evil in competition, but deem unrestricted competition to be as necessary to the health of the industrial and social organism as the free circulation of the blood is to the health of the bodily organism—to be the agency whereby the fullest co-operation is to be secured. We would simply take for the community what belongs to the community, the value that attaches to land by the growth of the community; leave sacredly to the individual all that belongs to the individual; and, treating necessary monopolies as functions of the state, abolish all restrictions and prohibitions save those required for public health, safety, morals and convenience.

But the fundamental difference—the difference I ask your Holiness specially to note, is in this: socialism in all its phases looks on the evils of our civilization as springing from the inadequacy or inharmony of natural relations, which must be artificially organized or improved. In its idea there devolves on the state the necessity of intelligently organizing the industrial relations of men; the construction, as it were, of a great machine whose complicated parts shall properly work together under the direction of human intelligence.

This is the reason why socialism tends towards atheism. Failing to see the order and symmetry of natural law, it fails to recognize God.

On the other hand, we who call ourselves single tax men (a name which expresses merely our practical propositions) see in the social and industrial relations of men not a machine which requires construction, but an organism which needs only to be suffered to grow. We see in the natural social and industrial laws such harmony as we see in the adjustments of the human body, and that as far transcends the power of man's intelligence to order and direct as it is beyond man's intelligence to order and direct the vital movements of his frame. We see in these social and industrial laws so close a relation to the moral law as must spring from the same Authorship, and that proves the moral law to be the sure guide of man where his intelligence would wander and go astray. Thus, to us, all that is needed to remedy the evils of our time is to do justice and give freedom. This is the reason why our beliefs tend towards, nay are indeed the only beliefs consistent with a firm and reverent faith in God, and with the recognition of His law as the supreme law which men must follow if they would secure prosperity and avoid destruction. This is the reason why to us political economy only serves to show the depth of wisdom in the simple truths which common people heard gladly from the lips of Him of whom it was said with wonder, "Is not this the Carpenter of Nazareth?"

And it is because that in what we propose—the securing to all men of equal natural opportunities for the exercise of their powers and the removal of all legal restriction on the legitimate exercise of those powers—we see the conformation of human law to the moral law, that we hold with confidence not merely that this is the sufficient remedy for all the evils you so strikingly portray, but that it is the only possible remedy.

Nor is there any other. The organization of man is such, his relations to the world in which he is placed are such—that is to say, the immutable laws of God are such, that it is beyond the power of human ingenuity to devise any way by which the evils born of the injustice that robs men of their birthright can be removed otherwise than by doing justice, by opening to all the bounty that God has provided for all.

Since man can live only on land and from land, since land is the reservoir of matter and force from which man's body itself is taken, and on which he must draw for all that he can produce, does it not irresistibly follow that to give the land in ownership to some men and to deny to others all right to it is to divide mankind into the rich and the poor, the privileged and the helpless? Does it not follow that those who have no rights to the use of land can live only by selling their power to labor to those who own the land? Does it not follow that what the socialists call "the iron law of wages," what the political economists term "the tendency of wages to a minimum," must take from the landless masses—the mere laborers, who of themselves have no power to use their labor—all the benefits of any possible advance or improvement that does not alter this unjust division of land. For having no power to employ themselves, they must, either as labor sellers or land renters, compete with one another for permission to labor. This competition with one another of men shut out from God's inexhaustible storehouse has no limit but starvation, and must ultimately force wages to their lowest point, the point at which life can just be maintained and reproduction carried on.

This is not to say that all wages must fall to this point, but that the wages of that necessarily largest stratum of laborers who have only ordinary knowledge, skill and aptitude must so fall. The wages of special classes, who are fenced off from the pressure of competition by peculiar knowledge, skill or other causes, may remain above that ordinary level. Thus, where the ability to read and write is rare its possession enables a man to obtain higher wages than the ordinary laborer. But as the diffusion of education makes the ability to read and write general this advantage is lost. So when a vocation requires special training or skill, or is made difficult of access by artificial restrictions, the checking of competition tends to keep wages in it at a higher level. But as the progress of invention dispenses with peculiar skill, or artificial restrictions are broken down, these higher wages sink to the ordinary level. And so, it is only so long as they are special that such qualities as industry, prudence and thrift can enable the ordinary laborer to maintain a condition above that which gives a mere living. Where they become general, the law of competition must reduce the earnings or savings of such qualities to the general level—which, land being monopolized and labor helpless, can be only that at which the next lowest point is the cessation of life.

Or, to state the same thing in another way: Land being necessary to life and labor, its owners will be able, in return for permission to use it, to obtain from mere laborers all that labor can produce, save enough to enable such of them to maintain life as are wanted by the land owners and their dependents.

Thus, where private property in land has divided society into a land owning class and a landless class, there is no possible invention or improvement, whether it be industrial, social or moral, which, so long as it does not affect the ownership of land, can prevent poverty or relieve the general conditions of mere laborers. For whether the effect of any invention or improvement be to increase what labor can produce or to decrease what is required to support the laborer, it can, so soon as it becomes general, result only in increasing the income of the owners of land, without at all benefiting the mere laborers. In no event can those possessed of the mere ordinary power to labor, a power utterly useless without the means necessary to labor, keep more of their earnings than enough to enable them to live.

How true this is we may see in the facts of to-day. In our own time invention and discovery have enormously increased the productive power of labor, and at the same time greatly reduced the cost of many things necessary to the support of the laborer. Have these improvements anywhere raised the earnings of the mere laborer? Have not their benefits mainly gone to the owners of land—enormously increased land values?

I say mainly, for some part of the benefit has gone to the cost of monstrous standing armies and warlike preparations; to the payment of interest on great public debts; and, largely disguised as interest on fictitious capital, to the owners of monopolies other than that of land. But improvements that would do away with these wastes would not benefit labor; they would simply increase the profits of land owners. Were standing armies and all their incidents abolished, were all monopolies other than that of land done away with, were governments to become models of economy, were the profits of speculators, of middlemen, of all sorts of exchangers saved, were every one to become so strictly honest that no policemen, no courts, no prisons, no precautions against dishonesty would be needed—the result would not differ from that which has followed the increase of productive power.

Nay, would not these very blessings bring starvation to many of those who now manage to live? Is it not true that if there were proposed to-day, what all Christian men ought to pray for, the complete disbandment of all the armies of Europe, the greatest fears would be aroused for the consequences of throwing on the labor market so many unemployed laborers?

The explanation of this and of similar paradoxes that in our time perplex on every side may be easily seen. The effect of all inventions and improvements that increase productive power, that save waste and economize effort, is to lessen the labor required for a given result, and thus to save labor, so that we speak of them as labor saving inventions or improvements. Now, in a natural state of society where the rights of all to the use of the earth are acknowledged, labor saving improvements might go to the very utmost that can be imagined without lessening the demand for men, since in such natural conditions the demand for men lies in their own enjoyment of life and the strong instincts that the Creator has implanted in the human breast. But in that unnatural state of society where **the masses of** men are disinherited of **all** but the **power to labor when** opportunity to labor **is given them** by others, there **the demand for them** becomes simply the demand for their services **by those who** hold this opportunity, and **man himself becomes** a commodity. Hence, although **the natural effect of** labor saving improvement is to increase wages, yet in **the** unnatural condition which private ownership of the land begets, the effect, even of such moral **improvements** as the disbandment **of armies** and the saving **of** the labor that **vice entails,** is by lessening the **commercial** demand, **to lower wages** and reduce mere **laborers to starvation** or pauperism. If labor saving **inventions and** improvements **could be** carried to the **very abolition of the** necessity for labor, what would **be the result? Would it not be** that land owners **could then get all** the wealth that the land was **capable of producing, and would have no need at all for laborers, who must then either starve or live as pensioners on the bounty of the land owners?**

Thus, **so** long as private property **in land continues** —**so long as** some men are treated as owners **of the** earth and other men can live on it only by their sufferance—human wisdom can devise no means by which the evils of our present condition may be avoided.

Nor yet could the **wisdom of God.**

By the **light of that** right reason of **which St. Thomas speaks we may see** that even He, the Almighty, **so long as His** laws remain what **they are,** could do nothing to prevent poverty and starvation while property in land continues.

How could He? Should he infuse new vigor into the sunlight, new virtue into the air, new fertility into the soil, would not all this new bounty go to the owners of the land, and work not benefit, but rather injury, to mere laborers? Should He open the minds of men to the possibilities of new substances, new adjustments, new powers, could this do any more to relieve poverty than steam, electricity and all the numberless discoveries and inventions of our time have done? Or, if He were to send down from the heavens above or cause to gush up from the subterranean depths, food, clothing, all the things that satisfy man's material desires, to whom under our laws would all these belong? So far from benefiting man, would not this increase and extension of His bounty prove but a curse, enabling the privileged class more riotously to roll in wealth, and bringing the disinherited class to more widespread starvation or pauperism?

IV.

Believing that the social question is at bottom a religious question, we deem it of happy augury to the world that in your Encyclical the most influential of all religious teachers has directed attention to the condition of labor.

But while we appreciate the many wholesome truths you utter, while we feel, as all must feel, that you are animated by a desire to help the suffering and oppressed, and to put an end to any idea that the Church is divorced from the aspiration for liberty and progress, yet it is painfully obvious to us that one fatal assumption hides from you **the cause** of the evils you see, and makes it impossible for you to propose any adequate remedy. This assumption is, that **private property** in land **is of** the same nature and has **the same sanctions as** private **property in** things produced by labor. In spite of its undeniable **truths and** its benevolent spirit, your Encyclical shows **you to be** involved in such difficulties **as a** physician **called to** examine one suffering from disease of the stomach would meet should **he** begin with a refusal to consider the stomach.

Prevented by this assumption **from seeing** the **true cause, the only causes you find it** possible to assign for the growth of misery and wretchedness are the **destruction of** workingmen's **guilds in the last century,** the repudiation in public institutions and **laws of** the ancient religion, rapacious usury, the custom of working by contract, and the concentration of trade.

Such diagnosis is manifestly inadequate to account **for evils that are alike felt** in Catholic countries, in Protestant countries, **in** countries that **adhere to the Greek communion and in** countries where **no religion is professed by the state;** that are alike **felt in old** countries and **in new countries; where industry** is simple and where it is **most elaborate; and amid all** varieties of industrial customs and relations.

But the real cause will be clear if you **will** consider that since labor must find its workshop and reservoir **in land, the labor question is** but another name for **the land question, and will** re-examine your assumption that private property in land is necessary and **right.**

See how fully adequate is the cause **I have pointed**

out. The most important of all the material relations of man is his relation to the planet he inhabits, and hence, the "impious resistance to the benevolent intentions of his Creator," which, as Bishop Nulty says, is involved in private property in land, *must* produce evils wherever it exists. But by virtue of the law, "unto whom much is given, from him much is required," the very progress of civilization makes the evils produced by private property in land more widespread and intense.

What is producing throughout the civilized world that condition of things you rightly describe as intolerable is not this and that local error or minor mistake. It is nothing less than the progress of civilization itself; nothing less than the intellectual advance and the material growth in which our century has been so pre-eminent, acting in a state of society based on private property in land; nothing less than the new gifts that in our time God has been showering on man, but which are being turned into scourges by man's "impious resistance to the benevolent intention of his Creator."

The discoveries of science, the gains of invention, have given to us in this wonderful century more than has been given to men in any time before; and, in a degree so rapidly accelerating as to suggest geometrical progression, are placing in our hands new material powers. But with the benefit comes the obligation. In a civilization beginning to pulse with steam and electricity, where the sun paints pictures and the phonograph stores speech, it will not do to be merely as just as were our fathers. Intellectual advance and material advance require corresponding moral advance. Knowledge and power are neither good nor evil. They are not ends but means—evolving forces that if not controlled in orderly relations must take disorderly and destructive forms. The deepening pain, the increasing perplexity, the growing discontent for which, as you truly say, *some remedy must be found and quickly found*, mean nothing less than that forces of destruction swifter and more terrible than those that have shattered every preceding civilization are already menacing ours —that if it does not quickly rise to a higher moral level; if it does not become in deed as in word a Christian civilization, on the wall of its splendor must flame the doom of Babylon: "Thou art weighed in the balance and found wanting!"

One false assumption prevents you from seeing the real cause and true significance of the facts that have prompted your Encyclical. And it fatally fetters you when you seek a remedy.

You state that you approach the subject with confidence, yet in all that greater part of the Encyclical (19–67) devoted to the remedy, while there is an abundance of moral reflections and injunctions, excellent in themselves but dead and meaningless as you apply them, the only definite practical proposals for the improvement of the condition of labor are:

1. That the State should step in to prevent overwork, to restrict the employment of women and children, to secure in workshops conditions not unfavorable to health and morals, and, at least where there is danger of insufficient wages provoking strikes, to regulate wages (39–40).

2. That it should encourage the acquisition of property (in land) by workingmen (50-51).

3. That workingmen's associations should be formed (52-67).

These remedies so far as they go are socialistic, and though the Encyclical is not without recognition of the individual character of man and of the priority of the individual and the family to the state, yet the whole tendency and spirit of its remedial suggestions lean unmistakably to socialism—extremely moderate socialism it is true; socialism hampered and emasculated by a supreme respect for private possessions; yet socialism still. But, although you frequently use the ambiguous term "private property" when the context shows that you have in mind private property in land, the one thing clear on the surface and becoming clearer still with examination is that you insist that whatever else may be done, the private ownership of land shall be left untouched.

I have already referred generally to the defects that attach to all socialistic remedies for the evil condition of labor, but respect for your Holiness dictates that I should speak specifically, even though briefly, of the remedies proposed or suggested by you.

Of these, the widest and strongest are that the state should restrict the hours of labor, the employment of women and children, the unsanitary conditions of workshops, etc. Yet how little may in this way be accomplished.

A strong, absolute ruler might hope by such regulations to alleviate the conditions of chattel slaves. But the tendency of our times is towards democracy, and democratic states are necessarily weaker in paternalism, while in the industrial slavery, growing out of private ownership of land, that prevails in Christendom to-day, it is not the master who forces the slave to labor, but the slave who urges the master to let him labor. Thus the greatest difficulty in enforcing such regulations comes from those whom they are intended to benefit. It is not, for instance, the masters who make it difficult to enforce restrictions on child labor in factories, but the mothers, who, prompted by poverty, misrepresent the ages of their children even to the masters, and teach the children to misrepresent.

But while in large factories and mines regulations as to hours, ages, etc., though subject to evasion and offering opportunities for extortion and corruption, may be to some extent enforced, how can they have any effect in those far wider branches of industry where the laborer works for himself or for small employers?

All such remedies are of the nature of the remedy for overcrowding that is generally prescribed with them—the restriction under penalty of the number who may occupy a room and the demolition of unsanitary buildings. Since these measures have no tendency to increase house accommodation or to augment ability to pay for it, the overcrowding that is forced back in some places goes on in other places and to a worse degree. All such remedies begin at the wrong end. They are like putting on brake and bit to hold in quietness horses that are being lashed into frenzy; they are like trying to stop a locomotive by holding its wheels instead of shutting off steam; like attempting to cure smallpox by driving back its pustules.

Men do not overwork themselves because they like it; it is not in the nature of the mother's heart to send children to work when they ought to be at play; it is not of choice that laborers will work in dangerous and unsanitary conditions. These things, like overcrowding, come from the sting of poverty. And so long as the poverty of which they are the expression is left untouched, restrictions such as you endorse can have only partial and evanescent results. The cause remaining, repression in one place can only bring out its effects in other places, and the task you assign to the state is as hopeless as to ask it to lower the level of the ocean by bailing out the sea.

Nor can the state cure poverty by regulating wages. It is as much beyond the power of the state to regulate wages as it is to regulate the rates of interest. Usury laws have been tried again and again, but the only effect they have ever had has been to increase what the poorer borrowers must pay, and for the same reasons that all attempts to lower by regulation the price of goods have always resulted merely in increasing them. The general rate of wages is fixed by the ease or difficulty with which labor can obtain access to land, ranging from the full earnings of labor, where land is free, to the least on which laborers can live and reproduce, where land is fully monopolized. Thus, where it has been comparatively easy for laborers to get land, as in the United States and in Australasia, wages have been higher than in Europe and it has been impossible to get European laborers to work there for wages that they would gladly accept at home; while as monopolization goes on under the influence of private property in land, wages tend to fall, and the social conditions of Europe to appear. Thus, under the partial yet substantial recognition of common rights to land, of which I have spoken, the many attempts of the British parliaments to reduce wages by regulation failed utterly. And so, when the institution of private property in land had done its work in England, all attempts of Parliament to raise wages proved unavailing. In the beginning of this century it was even attempted to increase the earnings of laborers by grants in aid of wages. But the only result was to lower commensurately what wages employers paid.

The state could only maintain wages above the tendency of the market (for as I have shown labor deprived of land becomes a commodity), by offering employment to all who wish it; or by lending its sanction to strikes and supporting them with its funds. Thus it is, that the thorough going socialists who want the state to take all industry into its hands are much more logical than those timid socialists who propose that the state should regulate private industry—but only a little.

The same hopelessness attends your suggestion that working people should be encouraged by the state in obtaining a share of the land. It is evident that by this you mean that, as is now being attempted in Ireland, the state shall buy out large land owners in favor of small ones, establishing what is known as peasant proprietors. Supposing that this can be done even to a considerable extent, what will be accomplished save to substitute a larger privileged class for a smaller privileged class? What will be done for the still larger class that must remain, the laborers of the agricultural districts, the workmen of the towns, the proletarians of the cities? Is it not true, as Professor De Laveleye says, that in such countries as Belgium, where peasant proprietary exists, the tenants, for there still exist tenants, are rackrented with a mercilessness unknown in Ireland? Is it not true that in such countries as Belgium the condition of the mere laborer is even worse than it is in Great Britain, where large ownerships obtain? And if the state attempts to buy up land for peasant proprietors will not the effect be, what is seen to-day in Ireland, to increase the market value of land and thus make it more difficult for those not so favored, and for those who will come after, to get land? How, moreover, on the principle which you declare (36), that "to the state the interests of all are equal, whether high or low," will you justify state aid to one man to buy a bit of land without also insisting on state aid to another man to buy a donkey, to another to buy a shop, to another to buy the tools and materials of a trade—state aid in short to everybody who may be able to make good use of it or thinks that he could? And are you not thus landed in communism—not the communism of the early Christians and of the religious orders, but communism that uses the coercive power of the state to take rightful property by force from those who have, to give to those who have not? For the state has no purse of Fortunatus; the state cannot repeat the miracle of the loaves and fishes; all that the state can give, it must get by some form or other of the taxing power. And whether it gives or lends money, or gives or lends credit, it cannot give to those who have not, without taking from those who have.

But aside from all this, any scheme of dividing up land while maintaining private property in land is futile. Small holdings cannot co-exist with the treatment of land as private property where civilization is materially advancing and wealth augments. We may see this in the economic tendencies that in ancient times were the main cause that transformed world-conquering Italy from a land of small farms to a land of great estates. We may see it in the fact that while two centuries ago the majority of English farmers were owners of the land they tilled, tenancy has been for a long time the all but universal condition of the English farmer. And now the mighty forces of steam and electricity have come to urge concentration. It is in the United States that we may see on the largest scale how their power is operating to turn a nation of land owners into a nation of tenants. The principle is clear and irresistible. Material progress makes land more valuable, and when this increasing value is left to private owners land must pass from the ownership of the poor into the ownership of the rich, just as diamonds so pass when poor men find them. What the British government is attempting in Ireland is to build snow houses in the Arabian desert! to plant bananas in Labrador!

There is one way, and only one way, in which working people in our civilization may be secured a share in the land of their country, and that is the way that we propose—the taking of the profits of land ownership for the community.

As to workingmen's associations, what your Holiness seems to contemplate is the formation and encouragement of societies akin to the Catholic sodalities, and to the friendly and beneficial societies, like the Odd Fellows, which have had a large extension in English speaking countries. Such associations may promote fraternity, extend social intercourse and provide assurance in case of sickness or death, but if they go no further they are powerless to affect wages even among their members. As to trades unions proper, it is hard to define your position, which is, perhaps, best stated as one of warm approbation provided that they do not go too far. For while you object to strikes; while you reprehend societies that "do their best to get into their hands the whole field of labor and to force workingmen either to join them or to starve;" while you discountenance the coercing of employers and seem to think that arbitration might take the place of strikes; yet you use expressions and assert principles that are all that the trade unionist would ask, not merely to justify the strike and the boycott, but even the use of violence where only violence would suffice. For you speak of the insufficient wages of workmen as due to the greed of rich employers; you assume the moral right of the workman to obtain employment from others at wages greater than those others are willing freely to give; and you deny the right of any one to work for such wages as he pleases, in such a way as to lead Mr. Stead, in so widely read a journal as the *Review of Reviews*, to approvingly declare that you regard " blacklegging," *i. e.*, the working for less than union wages, as a crime.

To men conscious of bitter injustice, to men steeped

in poverty yet mocked by flaunting wealth, such words mean more than I can think you realize.

When fire shall be cool and ice be warm, when armies shall throw away lead and iron, to try conclusions by the pelting of rose leaves, such labor associations as you are thinking of may be possible. But not till then. For labor associations can do nothing to raise wages but by force. It may be force applied passively, or force applied actively, or force held in reserve, but it must be force. They *must* coerce or hold the power to coerce employers; they *must* coerce those among their own members disposed to straggle; they *must* do their best to get into their hands the whole field of labor they seek to occupy and to force other workingmen either to join them or to starve. Those who tell you of trades unions bent on raising wages by moral suasion alone are like those who would tell you of tigers that live on oranges.

The condition of the masses to-day is that of men pressed together in a hall where ingress is open and more are constantly coming, but where the doors for egress are closed. If forbidden to relieve the general pressure by throwing open those doors, whose bars and bolts are private property in land, they can only mitigate the pressure on themselves by forcing back others, and the weakest must be driven to the wall. This is the way of labor unions and trade guilds. Even those amiable societies that you recommend would in their efforts to find employment for their own members necessarily displace others.

For even the philanthropy which, recognizing the evil of trying to help labor by alms, seeks to help men to help themselves by finding them work, becomes aggressive in the blind and bitter struggle that private property in land entails, and in helping one set of men injures others. Thus, to minimize the bitter complaints of taking work from others and lessening the wages of others in providing their own beneficiaries with work and wages, benevolent societies are forced to devices akin to the digging of holes and filling them up again. Our American societies feel this difficulty, General Booth encounters it in England, and the Catholic societies which your Holiness recommends must find it, when they are formed.

Your Holiness knows of, and I am sure honors, the princely generosity of Baron Hirsch towards his suffering co-religionists. But, as I write, the New York newspapers contain accounts of an immense meeting held in Cooper Union, in this city, on the evening of Friday, September 4, in which a number of Hebrew trades unions protested in the strongest manner against the loss of work and reduction of wages that is being effected by Baron Hirsch's generosity in bringing their own countrymen here and teaching them to work. The resolution unanimously adopted at this great meeting thus concludes:

"We now demand of Baron Hirsch himself that he release us from his 'charity' and take back the millions, which, instead of a blessing, have proved a curse and a source of misery."

Nor does this show that the members of these Hebrew labor unions—who are themselves immigrants of the same class as those Baron Hirsch is striving to help, for in the next generation they lose with us their distinctiveness—are a whit less generous than other men.

Labor associations of the nature of trade guilds or unions are necessarily selfish; by the law of their being they must fight for their own hand, regardless of who is hurt; they ignore and must ignore the teaching of Christ that we should do to others as we would have them do to us, which a true political economy shows is the only way to the full emancipation of the masses. They must do their best to starve workmen who do not join them, they must by all means in their power force back the "blackleg"—as the soldier in battle must shoot down his mother's son if in the opposing ranks. And who is the blackleg? A fellow creature seeking work—a fellow creature in all probability more pressed and starved than those who so bitterly denounce him, and often with the hungry pleading faces of wife and child behind him.

And, in so far as they succeed, what is it that trades guilds and unions do but to impose more restrictions on natural rights; to create "trusts" in labor; to add to privileged classes other somewhat privileged classes; and to press the weaker closer to the wall?

I speak without prejudice against trades unions, of which for years I was an active member. And in pointing out to your Holiness that their principle is selfish and incapable of large and permanent benefits, and that their methods violate natural rights and work hardship and injustice, I am only saying to you what, both in my books and by word of mouth, I have said over and over again to them. Nor is what I say capable of dispute. Intelligent trades unionists know it, and the less intelligent vaguely feel it. And even those of the classes of wealth and leisure who, as if to head off the demand for natural rights, are preaching trades unionism to working men, must needs admit it.

Your Holiness will remember the great London dock strike of two years ago, which, with that of other influential men, received the moral support of that Prince of the Church whom we of the English speech hold higher and dearer than any prelate has been held by us since the blood of Thomas A'Becket stained the Canterbury altar.

In a volume called "The Story of the Dockers' Strike," written by Messrs. H. Lewellyn Smith and Vaughan Nash, with an introduction by Sydney Buxton, M. P., which advocates trades unionism as the solution of the labor question, and of which a large number were sent to Australia as a sort of official recognition of the generous aid received from there by the strikers, I find in the summing up, on pages 164-5, the following:

"If the settlement lasts, work at the docks will be more regular, better paid, and carried on under better conditions than ever before. All this will be an unqualified gain to those who get the benefit from it. But another result will undoubtedly be *to contract the field of employment and lessen the number of those for whom work can be found.* The lower class casual will, in the end, find his position more precarious than ever before, in proportion to the increased regularity of work which the "fitter" of the laborers will secure. The effect of the organization of dock labor, as of all classes of labor, will be *to squeeze out the residuum.* The loafer, the cadger, the failure in the industrial race—the members of 'Class B' of Mr. Charles Booth's hierarchy of social classes—will be no gainers **by the** change, but will rather *find another door closed against them*, **and** this in many cases *the last **door** to employment*."

I **am far from** wishing that your Holiness should **join in** that pharisaical denunciation of trades unions common among those who, while quick to point out the injustice of trades unions in denying to others the **equal right to work**, are themselves supporters of that **more primary injustice that denies the** equal right to the standing place **and natural** material necessary to work. What I wish to point **out is** that trades unionism, while it may be a partial paliative, **is not a remedy; that it** has not that moral character **which could alone justify one in** the position of your Holiness in urging it **as good in** itself. Yet, so long as you insist on **private property in land** what better can you do?

V.

In the beginning **of** the Encyclical you declare that the responsibility of the apostolical office urges your Holiness to treat the question of the condition of labor " expressly and at length in **order** that there may **be no** mistake as to the principles **which truth and** justice dictate for its settlement." **But, blinded by** one false assumption, you do not see **even** fundamentals.

You assume that the labor **question is a** question between wage-workers and **their employers**. But working for wages is not the primary or exclusive occupation of **labor**. Primarily men **work** for **themselves** without **the** intervention **of an** employer. And the primary source of wages is in the earnings **of** labor, the man who works for himself and consumes his own products receiving his wages in the fruits of his labor. Are not fishermen, boatmen, cab drivers, peddlers, working farmers—all, in short, of the many workers who get their wages directly by the sale of their services or products without the medium of an employer, as much laborers as those who work for the specific wages of an employer? In your consideration of remedies you do not seem even to have thought of them. Yet in reality the laborers who work for themselves are the first to be considered, since what men will be willing to accept from employers depends manifestly on what they can get by working for themselves.

You assume that all employers are rich men, who might raise wages much higher were they not so grasping. But is it not the fact that the great majority of employers are in reality as much pressed by competition as their workmen, many of them constantly on the verge of failure? Such employers could not possibly raise the wages they pay, however they might wish to, unless all others were compelled to do so.

You assume that there are in the natural order two classes, the rich and the poor, and that laborers naturally belong to the poor.

It is true as you say that there are differences in capacity, in diligence, in health and in strength, that may produce differences in fortune. These, however, are not the differences that divide men into rich and poor. The natural differences in powers and aptitudes are certainly not greater than are natural differences in stature. But while it is only by selecting giants and dwarfs that we can find men twice as tall as others, yet in the difference between rich and poor that exists to-day we find some men richer than other men by the thousand fold and the million fold.

Nowhere do these differences between wealth and poverty coincide with differences in individual powers and aptitudes. The real difference between rich and poor is the difference between those who hold the toll gates and those who pay toll; between tribute receivers and tribute yielders.

In what way does nature justify such a difference? In the numberless varieties of animated nature we find some species that are evidently intended to live on other species. But their relations are always marked by unmistakable differences in size, shape or organs. To man has been given dominion over all the other living things that tenant the earth. But is not this mastery indicated even in externals, so that no one can fail on sight to distinguish between a man and one of the inferior animals. Our American apologists for slavery used to contend that the black skin and wooly hair of the negro indicated the intent of nature that the black should serve the white; but the difference that you assume to be natural is between men of the same race. What difference does nature show between such men as would indicate her intent that one should live idly yet be rich, and the other should work hard yet be poor? If I could bring you from the United States a man who has $200,000,000, and one who is glad to work for a few dollars a week, and place them side by side in your ante-chamber, would you be able to tell which was which, even were you to call in the most skilled anatomist? Is it not clear that

God in no way countenances or condones the division of rich and poor that exists to-day, or in any way permits it, except as having given them free will he permits men to choose either good or evil, and to avoid heaven if they prefer hell. For is it not clear that the division of men into the classes rich and poor has invariably its origin in force and fraud; invariably involves violation of the moral law; and is really a division into those who get the profits of robbery and those who are robbed; those who hold in exclusive possession what God made for all, and those who are deprived of His bounty? Did not Christ in all His utterances and parables show that the gross difference between rich and poor is opposed to God's law? Would he have condemned the rich so strongly as he did, if the class distinction between rich and poor did not involve injustice—was not opposed to God's intent?

It seems to us that your Holiness misses its real significance in intimating that Christ, in becoming the son of a carpenter and Himself working as a carpenter, showed merely that "there is nothing to be ashamed of in seeking one's bread by labor." To say that is almost like saying that by not robbing people He showed that there is nothing to be ashamed of in honesty? If you will consider how true in any large view is the classification of all men into workingmen, beggarmen and thieves, you will see that it was morally impossible that Christ during His stay on earth should have been anything else than a workingman, since He who came to fulfil the law must by deed as well as word obey God's law of labor.

See how fully and how beautifully Christ's life

on earth illustrated this law. Entering our earthly life in the weakness of infancy, as it is appointed that all should enter it, He lovingly took what in the natural order is lovingly rendered, the sustenance, secured by labor, that one generation owes to its immediate successors. Arrived at maturity, He earned His own subsistence by that common labor in which the majority of men must and do earn it. Then passing to a higher—to the very highest—sphere of labor, He earned His subsistence by the teaching of moral and spiritual truths, receiving its material wages in the love offerings of grateful hearers, and not refusing the costly spikenard with which Mary anointed His feet. So, when He chose His disciples, He did not go to land owners or other monopolists who live on the labor of others, but to common laboring men. And when He called them to a higher sphere of labor and sent them out to teach moral and spiritual truths, He told them to take, without condescension on the one hand or sense of degradation on the other, the loving return for such labor, saying to them that the "laborer is worthy of his hire," thus showing, what we hold, that all labor does not consist in what is called manual labor, but that whoever helps to add to the material, intellectual, moral or spiritual fullness of life is also a laborer.*

---

* Nor should it be forgotten that the investigator, the philosopher, the teacher, the artist, the poet, the priest, though not engaged in the production of wealth, are not only engaged in the production of utilities and satisfactions to which the production of wealth is only a means, but by acquiring and diffusing knowledge, stimulating mental powers and elevating the moral sense, may greatly increase the ability to produce wealth. For man does not live by bread alone. * * * He who by any exertion of mind or body adds to the aggregate of enjoyable wealth, increases the sum of human knowledge, or gives to human life higher eleva-

In assuming that laborers, even ordinary manual laborers, are naturally poor, you ignore the fact that labor is the producer of wealth, and attribute to the natural law of the Creator an injustice that comes from man's impious violation of His benevolent intention. In the rudest stage of the arts it is possible, where justice prevails, for all well men to earn a living. With the labor-saving appliances of our time, it should be possible for all to earn much more. And so, in saying that poverty is no disgrace, you convey an unreasonable implication. For poverty *ought* to be a disgrace, since in a condition of social justice, it would, where unsought from religious motives or unimposed by unavoidable misfortune, imply recklessness or laziness.

The sympathy of your Holiness seems exclusively directed to the poor, the workers. Ought this to be so? Are not the rich, the idlers, to be pitied also? By the word of the Gospel it is the rich rather than the poor who call for pity, for the presumption is that they will share the fate of Dives. And to any one who believes in a future life the condition of him who wakes to find his cherished millions left behind must seem pitiful. But even in this life, how really pitiable are the rich. The evil is not in wealth in itself—in its command over material things; it is in the possession

---

tion or greater fullness—he is, in the large meaning of the words, a "producer," a "working man," a "laborer," and is honestly earning honest wages. But he who without doing aught to make mankind richer, wiser, better, happier, lives on the toil of others— he, no matter by what name of honor he may be called, or how lustily the priests of Mammon may swing their censers before him, is in the last analysis but a beggarman or a thief.—Protection or Free Trade, pp. 74-75.

of wealth while others are steeped in poverty; in being raised above touch with the life of humanity, from its work and its struggles, its hopes and its fears, and above all, from the love that sweetens life, and the kindly sympathies and generous acts that strengthen faith in man and trust in God. Consider how the rich see the meaner side of human nature; how they are surrounded by flatterers and sycophants; how they find ready instruments not only to gratify vicious impulses, but to prompt and stimulate them; how they must constantly be on guard lest they be swindled; how often they must suspect an ulterior motive behind kindly deed or friendly word; how if they try to be generous they are beset by shameless beggars and scheming impostors; how often the family affections are chilled for them, and their deaths anticipated with the ill-concealed joy of expectant possession. The worst evil of poverty is not in the want of material things, but in the stunting and distortion of the higher qualities. So, though in another way, the possession of unearned wealth likewise stunts and distorts what is noblest in man.

God's commands cannot be evaded with impunity. If it be God's command that men shall earn their bread by labor, the idle rich must suffer. And they do. See the utter vacancy of the lives of those who live for pleasure; see the loathsome vices bred in a class who surrounded by poverty are sated with wealth. See that terrible punishment of *ennui*, of which the poor know so little that they cannot understand it; see the pessimism that grows among the wealthy classes— that shuts out God, that despises men, that deems existence in itself an evil, and fearing death yet longs for annihilation.

When Christ told the rich young man who sought Him to sell all he had and to give it to the poor, He was not thinking of the poor, but of the young man. And I doubt not that among the rich, and especially among the self-made rich, there are many who at times at least feel keenly the folly of their riches and fear for the dangers and temptations to which these expose their children. But the strength of long habit, the promptings of pride, the excitement of making and holding what has become for them the counters in a game of cards, the family expectations that have assumed the character of rights, and the real difficulty they find in making any good use of their wealth, bind them to their burden, like a weary donkey to his pack, till they stumble on the precipice that bounds this life.

Men who are sure of getting food when they shall need it eat only what appetite dictates. But with the sparse tribes who exist on the verge of the habitable globe life is either a famine or a feast. Enduring hunger for days, the fear of it prompts them to gorge like anacondas when successful in their quest of game. And so, what gives wealth its curse is what drives men to seek it, what makes it so envied and admired—the fear of want. As the unduly rich are the corollary of the unduly poor, so is the soul-destroying quality of riches but the reflex of the want that embrutes and degrades. The real evil lies in the injustice from which unnatural possession and unnatural deprivation both spring.

But this injustice can hardly be charged on individuals or classes. The existence of private property in land is a great social wrong from which society at large suffers, and of which the very rich and the very poor are alike victims, though at the opposite extremes. Seeing this, it seems to us like a violation of Christian charity to speak of the rich as though they individually were responsible for the sufferings of the poor. Yet, while you do this, you insist that the cause of monstrous wealth and degrading poverty shall not be touched. Here is a man with a disfiguring and dangerous excrescence. One physician would kindly, gently, but firmly remove it. Another insists that it shall not be removed, but at the same time holds up the poor victim to hatred and ridicule. Which is right?

In seeking to restore all men to their equal and natural rights we do not seek the benefit of any class, but of all. For we both know by faith and see by fact that injustice can profit no one and that justice must benefit all.

Nor do we seek any " futile and ridiculous equality." We recognize, with you, that there must always be differences and inequalities. In so far as these are in conformity with the moral law, in so far as they do not violate the command, " Thou shalt not steal," we are content. We do not seek to better God's work; we seek only to do His will. The equality we would bring about is not the equality of fortune, but the equality of natural opportunity; the equality that reason and religion alike proclaim—the equality in usufruct of all His children to the bounty of Our Father who art in Heaven.

And in taking for the uses of society what we

clearly see is the great fund intended for society in the divine order, we would not levy the slightest tax on the possessors of wealth, no matter how rich they might be. Not only do we deem such taxes a violation of the right of property, but we see that by virtue of beautiful adaptations in the economic laws of the Creator, it is impossible for any one honestly to acquire wealth, without at the same time adding to the wealth of the world.

To persist in a wrong, to refuse to undo it, is always to become involved in other wrongs. Those who defend private property in land, and thereby deny the first and most important of all human rights, the equal right to the material substratum of life, are compelled to one of two courses. Either they must, as do those whose gospel is "Devil take the hindermost," deny the equal right to life, and by some theory like that to which the English clergyman Malthus has given his name, assert that nature (they do not venture to say God) brings into the world more men than there is provision for; or, they must, as do the socialists, assert as rights what in themselves are wrongs.

Your Holiness in the Encyclical gives an example of this. Denying the equality of right to the material basis of life, and yet conscious that there is a right to live, you assert the right of laborers to employment and their right to receive from their employers a certain indefinite wage. No such rights exist. No one has a right to demand employment of another, or to demand higher wages than the other is willing to give, or in any way to put pressure on another to make him raise such wages against his will. There can be no better moral justification for such demands on employers by workingmen than there would be for employers demanding that workingmen shall be compelled to work for them when they do not want to and to accept wages lower than they are willing to take. Any seeming justification springs from a prior wrong, the denial to workingmen of their natural rights, and can in the last analysis only rest on that supreme dictate of self-preservation that under extraordinary circumstances makes pardonable what in itself is theft, or sacrilege or even murder.

A fugitive slave with the bloodhounds of his pursuers baying at his heels would in true Christian morals be held blameless if he seized the first horse he came across, even though to take it he had to knock down the rider. But this is not to justify horse-stealing as an ordinary means of traveling.

When his disciples were hungry Christ permitted them to pluck corn on the Sabbath day. But He never denied the sanctity of the Sabbath by asserting that it was under ordinary circumstances a proper time to gather corn.

He justified David, who when pressed by hunger committed what ordinarily would be sacrilege, by taking from the temple the loaves of proposition. But in this He was far from saying that the robbing of temples was a proper way of getting a living.

In the Encyclical however you commend the application to the ordinary relations of life, under normal conditions, of principles that in ethics are only to be tolerated under extraordinary conditions. You are driven to this assertion of false rights by your denial of true rights. The natural right which each man has is not that of demanding employment or wages from another man; but that of employing himself—that of applying by his own labor to the inexhaustible storehouse which the Creator has in the land provided for all men. Were that storehouse open, as by the single tax we would open it, the natural demand for labor would keep pace with the supply, the man who sold labor and the man who bought it would become free exchangers for mutual advantage, and all cause for dispute between workman and employer would be gone. For then, all being free to employ themselves, the mere opportunity to labor would cease to seem a boon; and since no one would work for another for less, all things considered, than he could earn by working for himself, wages would necessarily rise to their full value, and the relations of workman and employer be regulated by mutual interest and convenience.

This is the only way in which they can be satisfactorily regulated.

Your Holiness seems to assume that there is some just rate of wages that employers ought to be willing to pay and that laborers should be content to receive, and to imagine that if this were secured there would be an end of strife. This rate you evidently think of as that which will give workingmen a frugal living, and perhaps enable them by hard work and strict economy to lay by a little something.

But how can a just rate of wages be fixed without the "higgling of the market" any more than the just price of corn or pigs or ships or paintings can be so fixed? And would not arbitrary regulation in the one case as in the other check that interplay that most effectively promotes the economical adjustment of productive forces? Why should buyers of labor, any more than buyers of commodities, be called on to pay higher prices than in a free market they are compelled to pay? Why should the sellers of labor be content with anything less than in a free market they can obtain? Why should workingmen be content with frugal fare when the world is so rich? Why should they be satisfied with a life time of toil and stinting, when the world is so beautiful? Why should not they also desire to gratify the higher instincts, the finer tastes? Why should they be forever content to travel in the steerage when others find the cabin more enjoyable?

Nor will they. The ferment of our time does not arise merely from the fact that workingmen find it harder to live on the same scale of comfort. It is also and perhaps still more largely due to the increase of their desires with an improved scale of comfort. This increase of desire must continue. For workingmen are men. And man is the unsatisfied animal.

He is not an ox, of whom it may be said, so much grass, so much grain, so much water, and a little salt, and he will be content. On the contrary, the more he gets the more he craves. When he has enough food then he wants better food. When he gets a shelter then he wants a more commodious and tasty one. When his animal needs are satisfied then mental and spiritual desires arise.

This restless discontent is of the nature of man—of that nobler nature that raises him above the animals by so immeasurable a gulf, and shows him to be indeed created in the likeness of God. It is not to be quarrelled with, for it is the motor of all progress. It is this that has raised St. Peter's dome and on dull, dead canvass made the angelic face of the Madonna to glow; it is this that has weighed suns and analyzed stars, and opened page after page of the wonderful works of creative intelligence; it is this that has narrowed the Atlantic to an ocean ferry and trained the lightning to carry our messages to the remotest lands; it is this that is opening to us possibilities beside which all that our modern civilization has as yet accomplished seem small. Nor can it be repressed save by degrading and imbruting men; by reducing Europe to Asia.

Hence, short of what wages may be earned when all restrictions on labor are removed and access to natural opportunities on equal terms secured to all, it is impossible to fix any rate of wages that will be deemed just, or any rate of wages that can prevent workingmen striving to get more. So far from it making workingmen more contented to improve their condition a little, it is certain to make them more discontented.

Nor are you asking justice when you ask employers to pay their workingmen more than they are compelled to pay—more than they could get others to do the work for. You are asking charity. For the surplus that the rich employer thus gives is not in reality wages, it is essentially alms.

In speaking of the practical measures for the improvement of the condition of labor which your Holiness suggests, I have not mentioned what you place much stress upon—charity. But there is nothing practical in such recommendations as a cure for poverty, nor will any one so consider them. If it were possible for the giving of alms to abolish poverty there would be no poverty in Christendom.

Charity is indeed a noble and beautiful virtue, grateful to man and approved by God. But charity must be built on justice. It cannot supersede justice.

What is wrong with the condition of labor through the Christian world is that labor is robbed. And while you justify the continuance of that robbery it is idle to urge charity. To do so—to commend charity as a substitute for justice, is indeed something akin in essence to those heresies, condemned by your predecessors, that taught that the Gospel had superseded the law, and that the love of God exempted men from moral obligations.

All that charity can do where injustice exists is here and there to somewhat mollify the effects of injustice. It cannot cure them. Nor is even what little it can do to mollify the effects of injustice without evil. For what may be called the superimposed, and in this sense, secondary virtues, work evil where the fundamental or primary virtues are absent. Thus sobriety is a virtue and diligence is a virtue. But a sober and diligent thief is all the more dangerous. Thus patience is a virtue. But patience under wrong is the condoning of wrong. Thus it is a virtue to seek knowledge and to endeavor to cultivate the mental powers. But the wicked man becomes more capable of evil by reason of his intelligence. Devils we always think of as intelligent.

And thus that pseudo charity that discards and

denies justice works evil. On the one side, it demoralizes its recipients, outraging that human dignity which as you say " God himself treats with reverence," and turning into beggars and paupers men who to become self supporting, self respecting citizens only need the restitution of what God has given them. On the other side, it acts as an anodyne to the consciences of those who are living on the robbery of their fellows, and fosters that moral delusion and spiritual pride that Christ doubtless had in mind when he said it was easier for a camel to pass through the eye of a needle than for a rich man to enter the kingdom of Heaven. For it leads men steeped in injustice, and using their money and their influence to bolster up injustice, to think that in giving alms they are doing something more than their duty towards man and deserve to be very well thought of by God, and in a vague way to attribute to their own goodness what really belongs to God's goodness. For consider: Who is the All-provider? Who is it that as you say, "owes to man a storehouse that shall never fail," and which " he finds only in the inexhaustible fertility of the earth." Is it not God? And when, therefore, men, deprived of the bounty of their God, are made dependent on the bounty of their fellow creatures, are not these creatures, as it were, put in the place of God, to take credit to themselves for paying obligations that you yourself say God owes?

But worse perhaps than all else is the way in which this substituting of vague injunctions to charity for the clear-cut demands of justice opens an easy means for the professed teachers of the Christian religion of all branches and communions to placate Mammon while persuading themselves that they are serving God. Had the English clergy not subordinated the teaching of justice to the teaching of charity—to go no further in illustrating a principle of which the whole history of Christendom from Constantine's time to our own is witness—the Tudor tyranny would never have arisen, and the separation of the Church been averted; had the clergy of France never substituted charity for justice, the monstrous iniquities of the ancient regime would never have brought the horrors of the Great Revolution; and in my own country had those who should have preached justice not satisfied themselves with preaching kindness, chattel slavery could never have demanded the holocaust of our civil war.

No, your Holiness; as faith without works is dead, as men cannot give to God His due while denying to their fellows the rights He gave them, so charity unsupported by justice can do nothing to solve the problem of the existing condition of labor. Though the rich were to "bestow all their goods to feed the poor and give their bodies to be burned," poverty would continue while property in land continues.

Take the case of the rich man to-day who is honestly desirous of devoting his wealth to the improvement of the condition of labor. What can he do?

Bestow his wealth on those who need it? He may help some who deserve it, but will not improve general conditions. And against the good he may do will be the danger of doing harm.

Build churches? Under the shadow of churches poverty festers and the vice that is born of it breeds.

Build schools and colleges? Save as it may lead men to see the iniquity of private property in land, increased education can effect nothing for mere laborers, for as education is diffused the wages of education sink.

Establish hospitals? Why, already it seems to laborers that there are too many seeking work, and to save and prolong life is to add to the pressure.

Build model tenements? Unless he cheapens house accommodations he but drives further the class he would benefit, and *as* he cheapens house accommodation he brings more to seek employment and cheapens wages.

Institute laboratories, scientific schools, workshops for physical experiments? He but stimulates invention and discovery, the very forces that, acting on a society based on private property in land, are crushing labor as between the upper and the nether millstone.

Promote emigration from places where wages are low to places where they are somewhat higher? If he does, even those whom he at first helps to emigrate will soon turn on him to demand that such emigration shall be stopped as reducing their wages.

Give away what land he may have, or refuse to take rent for it, or let it at lower rents than the market price? He will simply make new land owners or partial land owners; he may make some individuals the richer, but he will do nothing to improve the general condition of labor.

Or, bethinking himself of those public spirited citizens of classic times who spent great sums in improving their native cities, shall he try to beautify the city of his birth or adoption? Let him widen and straighten narrow and crooked streets, let him build parks and erect fountains, let him open tramways and bring in railroads, or in any way make beautiful and attractive his chosen city, and what will be the result? Must it not be that those who appropriate God's bounty will take his also? Will it not be that the value of land will go up, and that the net result of his benefactions will be an increase of rents and a bounty to land owners? Why, even the mere announcement that he is going to do such things will start speculation and send up the value of land by leaps and bounds.

What, then, can the rich man do to improve the condition of labor?

He can do nothing at all except to use his strength for the abolition of the great primary wrong that robs men of their birthright. The justice of God laughs at the attempts of men to substitute anything else for it.

If when in speaking of the practical measures your Holiness proposes, I did not note the moral injunctions that the Encyclical contains, it is not because we do not think morality practical. On the contrary it seems to us that in the teachings of morality is to be found the highest practicality, and that the question, What is wise? may always safely be subordinated to the question, What is right? But your Holiness in the Encyclical expressly deprives the moral truths you state of all real bearing on the condition of labor, just as the American people, by their legalization of chattel slavery, used to deprive of all practical meaning the declaration they deem their fundamental charter, and were accustomed to read solemnly on every national anniversary. That declaration asserts that " We hold these truths to be self evident that all men are created equal and are endowed by their Creator with certain unalienable rights; that among these are life, liberty and the pursuit of happiness." But what did this truth mean on the lips of men who asserted that one man was the rightful property of another man who had bought him; who asserted that the slave was robbing the master in running away, and that the man or the woman who helped the fugitive to escape, or even gave him a cup of cold water in Christ's name, was an accessory to theft, on whose head the penalties of the state should be visited?

Consider the moral teachings of the Encyclical:

You tell us that God owes to man an inexhaustible storehouse which he finds only in the land. Yet you support a system that denies to the great majority of men all right of recourse to this storehouse.

You tell us that the necessity of labor is a consequence of original sin. Yet you support a system that exempts a privileged class from the necessity for labor and enables them to shift their share and much more than their share of labor on others.

You tell us that God has not created us for the perishable and transitory things of earth, but has given us this world as a place of exile and not as our true country. Yet you tell us that some of the exiles have the exclusive right of ownership in this place of common exile, so that they may compel their fellow exiles to pay *them* for sojourning here, and that this exclusive ownership they may transfer to other exiles yet to come, with the same right of excluding their fellows.

You tell us that virtue is the common inheritance of all; that all men are children of God the common Father; that all have the same last end; that all are redeemed by Jesus Christ; that the blessings of nature and the gifts of grace belong in common to all, and that to all except the unworthy is promised the inheritance of the Kingdom of Heaven! Yet in all this and through all this you insist as a moral duty on the maintenance of a system that makes the reservoir of all God's material bounties and blessings to man the exclusive property of a few of their number—you give us equal rights in heaven, but deny us equal rights on earth!

It was said of a famous decision of the Supreme Court of the United States made just before the civil war, in a fugitive slave case, that "it gave the law to the North and the nigger to the South." It is thus that your Encyclical gives the gospel to laborers and the earth to the landlords. Is it really to be wondered at that there are those who sneeringly say "The priests are ready enough to give the poor an equal share in all that is out of sight, but they take precious good care that the rich shall keep a tight grip on all that is within sight."

Herein is the reason why the working masses all over the world are turning away from organized religion.

And why should they not? What is the office of religion if not to point out the principles that ought to govern the conduct of men towards each other; to furnish a clear, decisive rule of right which shall guide men in all the relations of life—in the workshop, in the mart, in the forum and in the senate, as well as in the church; to supply, as it were, a compass by which amid the blasts of passion, the aberrations of greed and the delusions of a short-sighted expediency men may safely steer? What is the use of a religion that stands palsied and paltering in the face of the most momentous problems? What is the use of a religion that whatever it may promise for the next world can do nothing to prevent injustice in this? Early Christianity was not such a religion, else it would never have encountered the Roman persecutions; else it would never have swept the Roman world. The sceptical masters of Rome, tolerant of all gods, careless of what they deemed vulgar superstitions, were keenly sensitive to a doctrine based on equal rights; they feared instinctively a religion that inspired slave and proletarian with a new hope; that took for its central figure a crucified carpenter; that taught the equal fatherhood of God and the equal brotherhood of men; that looked for the speedy reign of justice, and that prayed, "*Thy Kingdom come on Earth!*"

To-day, the same perceptions, the same aspirations, exist among the masses. Man is, as he has been called, a religious animal, and can never quite rid himself of the feeling that there is some moral government of the world, some eternal distinction between wrong and right; can never quite abandon the yearning for a reign of righteousness. And to-day, men who, as they think, have cast off all belief in religion, will tell you, even though they know not what it is, that with regard to the condition of labor *some-*

thing is wrong! If theology be, as St. Thomas of Aquin held it, the sum and focus of the sciences, is it not the business of religion to say clearly and fearlessly what that wrong is? It was by a deep impulse that of old when threatened and perplexed by general disaster men came to the oracles to ask, In what have we offended the gods? To-day, menaced by growing evils that threaten the very existence of society, men, conscious that *something is wrong*, are putting the same question to the ministers of religion. What is the answer they get? Alas, with few exceptions, it is as vague, as inadequate, as the answers that used to come from heathen oracles.

Is it any wonder that the masses of men are losing faith?

Let me again state the case that your Encyclical presents:

What is that condition of labor which as you truly say is "the question of the hour," and "fills every mind with painful apprehension?" Reduced to its lowest expression it is the poverty of men willing to work. And what is the lowest expression of this phrase? It is that they lack bread—for in that one word we most concisely and strongly express all the manifold material satisfactions needed by humanity, the absence of which constitutes poverty.

Now what is the prayer of Christendom—the universal prayer: the prayer that goes up daily and hourly wherever the name of Christ is honored; that ascends from your Holiness at the high altar of St. Peter's, and that is repeated by the youngest child that the poorest Christian mother has taught to lisp a request to her Father in Heaven? It is, "Give us this day our daily bread!"

Yet where this prayer goes up, daily and hourly, men lack bread. Is it not the business of religion to say why? If it cannot do so, shall not scoffers mock its ministers as Elias mocked the prophets of Baal, saying, "Cry with a louder voice, for he is a god; and perhaps he is talking, or is in an inn, or on a journey or perhaps he is asleep, and must be awaked!" What answer can those ministers give? Either there is no God, or He is asleep, or else He does give men their daily bread, and it is in some way intercepted.

Here is the answer, the only true answer: If men lack bread it is not that God has not done His part in providing it. If men willing to labor are cursed with poverty, it is not that the storehouse that God owes men has failed; that the daily supply He has promised for the daily wants of His children is not here in abundance. It is, that impiously violating the benevolent intentions of their Creator, men have made land private property, and thus given into the exclusive ownership of the few the provision that a bountiful Father has made for all.

Any other answer than that, no matter how it may be shrouded in the mere forms of religion, is practically an atheistical answer.

I have written this letter not alone for your Holiness, but for all whom I may hope it to reach. But in sending it to you personally, and in advance of publication, I trust that it may be by you personally read and weighed. In setting forth the grounds of our belief and in pointing out considerations which **it seems** to us you have unfortunately overlooked, I have written frankly, as was my duty on a matter of such momentous importance, and as I am sure you would have me write. But I trust I have done so without offence. **For your office I have profound** respect, for **yourself personally the highest esteem.** And while the views I have opposed seem **to us** erroneous and dangerous, we **do** not wish to be **understood** as in the slightest degree questioning either your sincerity or intelligence in adopting them. For **they are views** all but universally held by the professed religious teachers of Christendom, in all communions **and creeds, and** that have received **the** sanction of those looked to as the wise and learned. Under the conditions that have surrounded you, and under the pressure of **so** many high duties and responsibilities, culminating in those of your present exalted position, it is not to be expected that **you** should have hitherto thought to question them. But I trust that the considerations herein set forth **may** induce you to do so, and even if the burdens and **cares that** beset you shall now make impossible **the** careful consideration that should precede expression **by one in** your responsible position I trust that what **I have written** may not be without use to others.

And, as I have said, we are deeply grateful for your Encyclical. It is much that by so conspicuously calling attention to the condition of labor, **you** have recalled the fact forgotten by so many that **the social evils** and problems of our time directly and **pressingly** concern the Church. It is much that you should thus have placed the stamp of your disapproval on that impious doctrine which directly and by implication has been so long and so widely preached in the name of Christianity, that the sufferings of the poor are due to mysterious decrees of Providence which men may lament but cannot alter. Your Encyclical will be seen by those who carefully analyze it to be directed not against socialism, which in moderate form you favor, but against what we in the United States call the single tax. Yet we have no solicitude for the truth save that it shall be brought into discussion, and we recognize in your Holiness' Encyclical a most efficient means of promoting discussion, and of promoting discussion along the lines that we deem of the greatest importance—the lines of morality and religion. In this you deserve the gratitude of all who would follow truth, for it is of the nature of truth always to prevail over error where discussion goes on.

And the truth for which we stand has now made such progress in the minds of men that it must be heard; that it can never be stifled; that it must go on conquering and to conquer. Far off Australia leads the van, and has already taken the first steps towards the single tax. In Great Britain, in the United States, and in Canada, the question is on the verge of practical politics and soon will be the burning issue of the time. Continental Europe cannot long linger behind. Faster than ever the world is moving.

Forty years ago slavery seemed stronger in the United States than ever before, and the market price of slaves—both working slaves and breeding slaves—

was higher than it had ever been before, for the title of the owner seemed growing more secure. In the shadow of the Hall where the equal rights of man had been solemnly proclaimed, the manacled fugitive was dragged back to bondage, and on what to American tradition was our Marathon of freedom, the slave master boasted that he would yet call the roll of his chattels.

Yet forty years ago, though the party that was to place Abraham Lincoln in the Presidential chair had not been formed, and nearly a decade was yet to pass ere the signal gun was to ring out, slavery, as we may now see, was doomed.

To-day a wider, deeper, more beneficent revolution is brooding, not over one country, but over the world. God's truth impels it, and forces mightier than He has ever before given to man urge it on. It is no more in the power of vested wrongs to stay it than it is in man's power to stay the sun. The stars in their courses fight against Sisera, and in the ferment of to-day, to him who hath ears to hear, the doom of industrial slavery is sealed.

Where shall the dignitaries of the Church be in the struggle that is coming, nay that is already here? On the side of justice and liberty, or on the side of wrong and slavery? with the delivered when the timbrels shall sound again, or with the chariots and the horsemen that again shall be engulfed in the sea?

As to the masses, there is little fear where they will be. Already, among those who hold it with religious fervor, the single tax counts great numbers of Catholics, many priests, secular and regular, and at least some bishops, while there is no communion or denomination of the many into which English speaking Christians are divided where its advocates are not to be found.

Last Sunday evening in the New York church that of all churches in the world is most richly endowed, I saw the cross carried through its aisles by a hundred choristers, and heard a priest of that English branch of the Church that three hundred years since was separated from your obedience, declare to a great congregation that the labor question was at bottom a religious question; that it could only be settled on the basis of moral right; that the first and clearest of rights is the equal right to the use of the physical basis of all life; and that no human titles could set aside God's gift of the land to all men.

And as the Cross moved by, and the choristers sang,

"Raise ye the Christian's war-cry—
The Cross of Christ the Lord!"

men to whom it was a new thing bowed their heads, and in hearts long steeled against the Church, as the willing handmaid of oppression, rose the "God wills it!" of the grandest and mightiest of crusades.

Servant of the Servants of God! I call you by the strongest and sweetest of your titles. In your hands more than in those of any living man lies the power to say the word and make the sign that shall end an unnatural divorce, and marry again to religion all that is pure and high in social aspiration

Wishing for your Holiness the chiefest of all blessings, that you may know the truth and be freed by the truth; **wishing for** you the days and the strength that may enable you by the **great** service **you** may render to humanity **to** make your pontificate through all coming time most glorious; and with the profound respect due to your personal character and to your exalted **office, I am,**

    Yours sincerely,

        HENRY GEORGE.

NEW YORK, September 11, 1891.

APPENDIX

Encyclical Letter

OF

POPE LEO XIII.

ON

THE CONDITION OF LABOR

OFFICIAL TRANSLATION

To our Venerable Brethren, all Patriarchs, Primates, Archbishops, and Bishops of the Catholic World, in grace and communion with the Apostolic See, Pope Leo XIII.

VENERABLE BRETHREN, HEALTH AND APOSTOLIC BENEDICTION.

1. It is not surprising that the spirit of revolutionary change, which has so long been predominant in the nations of the world, should have passed beyond politics and made its influence felt in the cognate field of practical economy. The elements of a conflict are unmistakable: the growth of industry, and the surprising discoveries of science; the changed relations of masters and workmen; the enormous fortunes of individuals, and the poverty of the masses; the increased self-reliance and the closer mutual combination of the working population; and, finally, a general moral deterioration. The momentous seriousness of the present state of things just now fills every mind with painful apprehension; wise men discuss it; practical men propose schemes; popular meetings, legislatures, and sovereign princes, all are occupied with it—and there is nothing which has a deeper hold on public attention.

2. Therefore, Venerable Brethren, as on former occasions, when it seemed opportune to refute false teaching, We have addressed you in the interest of the Church and of the common weal, and have issued Letters on Political Power, on Human Liberty, on the Christian Constitution of the State, and on similar subjects, so now we have thought it useful to speak on the CONDITION OF LABOR. It is a matter on which We

have touched once or twice already. But in this Letter the responsibility of the Apostolic office urges Us to treat the question expressly and at length, in order that there may be no mistake as to the principles which truth and justice dictate for its settlement. The discussion is not easy, nor is it free from danger. It is not easy to define the relative rights and the mutual duties of the wealthy and of the poor, of capital and of labor. And the danger lies in this, that crafty agitators constantly make use of these disputes to pervert men's judgments and to stir up the people to sedition.

3. But all agree, and there can be no question whatever, that some remedy must be found, and quickly found, for the misery and wretchedness which press so heavily at this moment on the large majority of the very poor. The ancient workmen's Guildes were destroyed in the last century, and no other organization took their place. Public institutions and the laws have repudiated the ancient religion. Hence by degrees it has come to pass that Working-Men have been given over, isolated and defenseless, to the callousness of employers, and the greed of unrestrained competition. The evil has been increased by rapacious Usury, which, although more than once condemned by the Church, is nevertheless, under a different form but with the same guilt, still practiced by avaricious and grasping men. And to this must be added the custom of working by contract, and the concentration of so many branches of trade in the hands of a few individuals, so that a small number of very rich men have been able to lay upon the masses of the poor a yoke little better than slavery itself.

4. To remedy these evils the *Socialists*, working on the poor man's envy of the rich, endeavor to destroy private property, and maintain that individual possessions should become the common property of all, to be administered by the State or by municipal bodies. They hold that, by thus transferring property from private persons to the community, the present evil state of things will be set to rights, because each citizen will then have his equal share of whatever there is to enjoy. But their proposals are so clearly futile for all practi-

cal purposes, that if they were carried out the workingman himself would be among the first to suffer. Moreover they are emphatically unjust, because they would rob the lawful possessor, bring the State into a sphere that is not its own, and cause complete confusion in the community.

5. It is surely undeniable that, when a man engages in remunerative labor, the very reason and motive of his work is to obtain property, and to hold it as his own private possession. If one man hires out to another his strength or his industry, he does this for the purpose of receiving in return what is necessary for food and living; he thereby expressly proposes to acquire a full and real right, not only to the remuneration, but also to the disposal of that remuneration as he pleases. Thus, if he lives sparingly, saves money, and invests his savings, for greater security, in land, the land in such a case is only his wages in another form; and consequently, a working man's little estate thus purchased should be as completely at his own disposal as the wages he receives for his labor. But it is precisely in this power of disposal that ownership consists, whether the property be land or movable goods. The *Socialists*, therefore, in endeavoring to transfer the possessions of individuals to the community, strike at the interests of every wage-earner, for they deprive him of the liberty of disposing of his wages, and thus of all hope and possibility of increasing his stock and of bettering his condition in life.

6. What is of still greater importance, however, is that the remedy they propose is manifestly against justice. For every man has by nature the right to possess property as his own. This is one of the chief points of distinction between man and the animal creation. For the brute has no power of self-direction, but is governed by two chief instincts, which keep his powers alert, move him to use his strength, and determine him to action without the power of choice. These instincts are self-preservation and the propagation of the species. Both can attain their purpose by means of things which are close at hand; beyond their surroundings the brute creation cannot go, for they are moved to action by

sensibility alone, and by the things which sense perceives. But with man it is different indeed. He possesses, on the one hand, the full perfection of animal nature, and therefore he enjoys, at least as much as the rest of the animal race, the fruition of the things of the body. But animality, however perfect, is far from being the whole of humanity, and is indeed humanity's humble handmaid, made to serve and obey. It is the mind, or the reason, which is the chief thing in us who are human beings; it is this which makes a human being human, and distinguishes him essentially and completely from the brute. And on this account—viz., that man alone among animals possesses reason—it must be within his right to have things not merely for temporary and momentary use, as other living beings have them, but in stable and permanent possession; he must have not only things which perish in the using, but also those which, though used, remain for use in the future.

7. This becomes still more clearly evident if we consider man's nature a little more deeply. For man, comprehending by the power of his reason things innumerable, and joining the future with the present—being, moreover, the master of his own acts—governs himself by the foresight of his counsel, under the eternal law and the power of God, Whose Providence governs all things; wherefore it is in his power to exercise his choice not only on things which regard his present welfare, but also on those which will be for his advantage in time to come. Hence man not only can possess the fruits of the earth, but also the earth itself; for of the products of the earth he can make provision for the future. Man's needs do not die out, but recur; satisfied to-day, they demand new supplies to-morrow. Nature, therefore, owes to man a storehouse that shall never fail, the daily supply of his daily wants. And this he finds only in the inexhaustible fertility of the earth.

8. Nor must we, at this stage, have recourse to the State. Man is older than the State; and he holds the right of providing for the life of his body prior to the formation of any State. And to say that God has given the earth to the use and enjoyment of the universal hu-

man race is not to deny that there can be private property. For God has granted the earth to mankind in general; not in the sense that all without distinction can deal with it as they please, but rather that no part of it has been assigned to any one in particular, and that the limits of private possession have been left to be fixed by man's own industry and the laws of individual peoples. Moreover the earth, though divided among private owners, ceases not thereby to minister to the needs of all; for there is no one who does not live on what the land brings forth. Those who do not possess the soil, contribute their labor; so that it may be truly said that all human subsistence is derived either from labor on one's own land, or from some laborious industry which is paid for either in the produce of the land itself or in that which is exchanged for what the land brings forth.

9. Here, again, we have another proof that private ownership is according to nature's law. For that which is required for the preservation of life, and for life's well being, is produced in great abundance by the earth, but not until man has brought it into cultivation and lavished upon it his care and skill. Now, when man thus spends the industry of his mind and the strength of his body in procuring the fruits of nature, by that act he makes his own that portion of nature's field which he cultivates—that portion on which he leaves, as it were, the impress of his own personality; and it cannot but be just that he should possess that portion as his own, and should have a right to keep it without molestation.

10. These arguments are so strong and convincing that it seems surprising that certain obsolete opinions should now be revived in opposition to what is here laid down. We are told that it is right for private persons to have the use of the soil and the fruits of their land, but that it is unjust for any one to possess as owner either the land on which he has built or the estate which he has cultivated. But those who assert this do not perceive that they are robbing man of what his own labor has produced. For the soil which is tilled and cultivated with toil and skill utterly changes its con-

dition; it was wild before, it is now fruitful ; it was barren, and now it brings forth in abundance. That which has thus altered and improved it becomes so truly part of itself as to be in great measure indistinguishable and inseparable from it. Is it just that the fruit of a man's sweat and labor should be enjoyed by another? As effects follow their cause, so it is just and right that the results of labor should belong to him who has labored.

11. With reason, therefore, the common opinion of mankind, little affected by the few dissentients who have maintained the opposite view, has found in the study of nature, and in the law of Nature herself, the foundation of the division of property, and has consecrated by the practice of all ages the principle of private ownership, as being pre-eminently in conformity with human nature, and as conducing in the most unmistakable manner to the peace and tranquility of human life. The same principle is confirmed and enforced by the civil laws—laws which, as long as they are just, derive their binding force from the law of nature. The authority of the Divine Law adds its sanction, forbidding us in the gravest terms even to covet that which is another's:—*Thou shalt not covet thy neighbor's wife; nor his house, nor his field, nor his man-servant, nor his maid-servant, nor his ox, nor his ass, nor anything which is his.**

12. The rights here spoken of, belonging to each individual man, are seen in a much stronger light if they are considered in relation to man's social and domestic obligations.

13. In choosing a state of life, it is indisputable that all are at full liberty either to follow the counsel of Jesus Christ as to the virginity, or to enter into the bonds of marriage. No human law can abolish the natural and primitive right of marriage, or in any way limit the chief and principal purpose of marriage, ordained by God's authority from the beginning : *Increase and multiply.* † Thus we have the Family ; the "society" of a man's own household ; a society limited

---

* Deuteronomy v., 21.   † Genesis i., 28.

indeed in numbers, but a true "society," anterior to every kind of State or nation, with rights and duties of its own, totally independent of the commonwealth.

14. That right of property, therefore, which has been proved to belong naturally to individual persons, must also belong to a man in his capacity of head of a family; nay, such a person must possess this right so much the more clearly in proportion as his position multiplies his duties. For it is a most sacred law of nature that a father must provide food and all necessaries for those whom he has begotten; and, similarly, nature dictates that a man's children, who carry on, as it were, and continue his own personality, should be provided by him with all that is needful to enable them honorably to keep themselves from want and misery in the uncertainties of this mortal life. Now, in no other way can a father effect this except by the ownership of profitable property, which he can transmit to his children by inheritance. A family, no less than a State, is, as We have said, a true society, governed by a power within itself, that is to say by the father. Wherefore, provided the limits be not transgressed which are prescribed by the very purposes for which it exists, the Family has at least equal rights with the State in the choice and pursuit of those things which are needful to its preservation and its just liberty.

15. We say, at least equal rights; for since the domestic household is anterior both in idea and in fact to the gathering of men into a commonwealth, the former must necessarily have rights and duties which are prior to those of the latter, and which rest more immediately on nature. If the citizens of a State—that is to say, the Families—on entering into association and fellowship, experienced at the hands of the State hindrance instead of help, and found their rights attacked instead of being protected, such association were rather to be repudiated than sought after.

16. The idea, then, that the civil government should, at its own discretion, penetrate and pervade the family and the household, is a great and pernicious mistake. True, if a family finds itself in great difficulty, utterly friendless, and without prospect of help, it is right

that extreme necessity be met by public aid ; for each family is a part of the commonwealth. In like manner, if within the walls of the household there occur grave disturbance of mutual rights, the public power must interfere to force each party to give the other what is due ; for this is not to rob citizens of their rights, but justly and properly to safeguard and strengthen them. But the rulers of the State must go no further : nature bids them stop here. Paternal authority can neither be abolished by the State, nor absorbed ; for it has the same source as human life itself. "The child belongs to the father," and is, as it were, the continuation of the father's personality ; and, to speak with strictness, the child takes its place in civil society not in its own right, but in its quality as a member of the family in which it is begotten. And it is for the very reason that "the child belongs to the father" that, as St. Thomas of Aquin says, "before it attains the use of free-will, it is in the power and care of its parents."* The Socialists, therefore, in setting aside the parent and introducing the providence of the State, act *against natural justice,* and threaten the very existence of family life.

17. And such interference is not only unjust, but it is quite certain to harass and disturb all classes of citizens and to subject them to odious and intolerable slavery. It would open the door to envy, to evil speaking, and to quarreling ; the sources of wealth would themselves run dry, for no one would have any interest in exerting his talents or his industry ; and that ideal equality of which so much is said would in reality be the levelling down of all to the same condition of misery and dishonor.

18. Thus it is clear that the main tenet of *Socialism,* the community of goods, must be utterly rejected ; for it would injure those whom it is intended to benefit, it would be contrary to the natural rights of mankind, and it would introduce confusion and disorder into the commonwealth. Our first and most fundamental principle, therefore, when we undertake to alleviate the condition

---

*St. Thomas, *Summa Theologica,* 2a 2æ Q. x. Art. 12.

of the masses, must be the inviolability of private property. This laid down, We go on to show where We must find the remedy that We seek.

19. We approach the subject with confidence, and in the exercise of the rights which belong to Us. For no practical solution of this question will ever be found without the assistance of Religion and of the Church. It is We who are the chief guardian of Religion and the chief dispenser of what belongs to the Church, and We must not by silence neglect the duty which lies upon Us. Doubtless this most serious question demands the attention and the efforts of others besides Ourselves— of the rulers of States, of employers of labor, of the wealthy, and of the working population themselves for whom We plead. But We affirm without hesitation, that all the striving of men will be vain if they leave out the Church. It is the Church that proclaims from the Gospel those teachings by which the conflict can be put an end to, or at the least made far less bitter; the Church uses its efforts not only to enlighten the mind, but to direct by its precepts the life and conduct of men; the Church improves and ameliorates the condition of the workingman by numerous useful organizations; does its best to enlist the services of all ranks in discussing and endeavoring to meet, in the most practical way, the claims of the working classes; and acts on the decided view that for these purposes recourse should be had, in due measure and degree, to the help of the law and of State authority.

20. Let it be laid down, in the first place, that humanity must remain as it is. It is impossible to reduce human society to a level. The *Socialists* may do their utmost, but all striving against nature is vain. There naturally exist among mankind innumerable differences of the most important kind; people differ in capability, in diligence, in health, and in strength; and unequal fortune is a necessary result of inequality in condition. Such inequality is far from being disadvantageous either to individuals or to the community; social and public life can only go on by the help of various kinds of capacity and the playing of many parts; and each man, as a rule, chooses the part

which peculiarly suits his case. As regards bodily labor, even had man never fallen from *the state of innocence*, he would not have been wholly unoccupied ; but that which would then have been his free choice and his delight, became afterwards compulsory, and the painful expiation of his sin. *Cursed be the earth in thy work ; in thy labor thou shalt eat of it all the days of thy life.** In like manner, the other pains and hardships of life will have no end or cessation on this earth ; for the consequences of sin are bitter and hard to bear, and they must be with man as long as life lasts. To suffer and to endure, therefore, is the lot of humanity ; let men try as they may, no strength and no artifice will ever succeed in banishing from human life the ills and troubles which beset it. If any there are who pretend differently—who hold out to a hard-pressed people freedom from pain and trouble, undisturbed repose, and constant enjoyment—they cheat the people and impose upon them, and their lying promises will only make the evil worse than before. There is nothing more useful than to look at the world as it really is— and at the same time to look elsewhere for a remedy to its troubles.

21. The great mistake that is made in the matter now under consideration is to possess one's self of the idea that class is naturally hostile to class ; that rich and poor are intended by nature to live at war with one another. So irrational and so false is this view, that the exact contrary is the truth. Just as the symmetry of the human body is the result of the disposition of the members of the body, so in a state it is ordained by nature that these two classes should exist in harmony and agreement, and should, as it were, fit into one another, so as to maintain the equilibrium of the body politic. Each requires the other ; capital cannot do without labor, nor labor without capital. Mutual agreement results in pleasantness and good order ; perpetual conflict necessarily produces confusion and outrage. Now, in preventing such strife as this, and in making it impossible, the efficacy of Christianity is

---

*Genesis iii., 17.

marvelous and manifold. First of all, there is nothing more powerful than Religion (of which the Church is the interpreter and guardian) in drawing rich and poor together, by reminding each class of its duties to the other, and especially of the duties of justice. Thus Religion teaches the laboring man and the workman to carry out honestly and well all equitable agreements freely made ; never to injure capital, or to outrage the person of an employer ; never to employ violence in representing his own cause, or to engage in riot or disorder ; and to have nothing to do with men of evil principles, who work upon the people with artful promises, and raise foolish hopes which usually end in disaster and in repentance when too late. Religion teaches the rich man and the employer that their work people are not their slaves ; that they must respect in every man his dignity as a man and as a Christian ; that labor is nothing to be ashamed of, if we listen to right reason and to Christian philosophy, but is an honorable employment, enabling a man to sustain his life in an upright and creditable way ; and that it is shameful and inhuman to treat men like chattels to make money by, or to look upon them merely as so much muscle or physical power. Thus, again, Religion teaches that, as among the workman's concerns are Religion herself and things spiritual and mental, the employer is bound to see that he has time for the duties of piety ; that he be not exposed to corrupting influences and dangerous occasions ; and that he be not led away to neglect his home and family or to squander his wages. Then, again, the employer must never tax his work people beyond their strength, nor employ them in work unsuited to their sex or age. His great and principal obligation is to give to every one that which is just. Doubtless before we can decide whether wages are adequate, many things have to be considered ; but rich men and masters should remember this—that to exercise pressure for the sake of gain upon the indigent and the destitute, and to make one's profit out of the need of another is condemned by all laws, human and divine. To defraud any one of wages that are his due is a crime which cries to the avenging anger of Heaven. *Behold*, *the hire of the laborers . . . which by fraud hath been kept back by you, crieth ; and the cry of them hath entered into the ears of the Lord of Sabaoth.** Finally, the rich must religiously refrain from cutting down the workman's earnings, either by force, by fraud, or by usurious dealing ; and with the more reason because the poor man is weak and unprotected, and because his slender means should be sacred in proportion to their scantiness.

22. Were these prospects carefully obeyed and followed, would not strife die out and cease?

23. But the Church, with Jesus Christ for its Master and Guide, aims higher still. It lays down precepts yet more perfect, and tries to bind class to class in friendliness and good understanding. The things of this earth cannot be understood or valued rightly without taking into consideration the life to come, the life that will last for ever. Exclude the idea of futurity, and the very notion of what is good and right would perish ; nay, the whole system of the universe would become a dark and unfathomable mystery. The great truth which we learn from Nature herself is also the grand Christain dogma on which Religion rests as on its base—that when we have done with this present life then shall we really begin to live. God has not created us for the perishable and transitory things of earth, but for things heavenly and everlasting ; He has given us this world as a place of exile, and not as our true country. Money, and the other things which men call good and desirable—we may have them in abundance, or we may want them altogether ; as far as eternal happiness is concerned, it is no matter ; the only thing that is important is to use them aright. Jesus Christ, when he redeemed us with *plentiful redemption*, took not away the pains and sorrows which in such large proportion make up the texture of our mortal life ; He transformed them into motives of virtue and occasions of merit ; and no man can hope for eternal reward unless he follow in the blood-stained footprints of his Saviour. *If we suffer with Him, we shall also reign*

---

* St. James v., 4.

with Him.* His labors and his sufferings, accepted by His own free-will, have marvelously sweetened all suffering and all labor. And not only by his example, but by His grace and by the hope of everlasting recompense, He has made pain and grief more easy to endure ; *for that which is at present momentary and light of our tribulation, worketh for us above measure exceedingly an eternal weight of glory.*†

24. Therefore those whom **fortune favors are warned that freedom from sorrow and** abundance **of earthly riches are no guarantee of** the **beatitude that shall never end, but rather the contrary ;**‡ **that the rich should tremble at the threatenings of Jesus Christ— threatenings so** strange **in** the **mouth of Our Lord ;** § **and that a most** strict account **must be given to the Supreme Judge for all that we possess.** The chiefest and most excellent rule for **the right use of money is** one which **the** heathen **philosophers indicated, but which the Church has traced out clearly, and has not only made known to men's minds, but has impressed upon their** lives. **It rests on the principle that it is one** thing **to** have a right **to the possession of money, and another to have a** right **to use money as one pleases. Private ownership, as we have seen, is the natural right of man ; and to exercise that** right, **especially as members of society, is not only** lawful, **but** absolutely **necessary. It is** *lawful,* **says St. Thomas of Aquin,** *for a man to hold private property ; and it is also necessary for the carrying on of human life.*‖ **But if the question be asked, How must one's possessions be used ? the Church replies without hesitation in the words of the same holy** Doctor : *Man* **should** *not consider his outward possessions as his own,* **but** *as common to all, so as to* **share** *them without difficulty* **when** others **are** *in need.* **Whence the** Apostle saith, Command the **rich** *of this world . . . to give with* **ease, to communicate.**¶ **True no one is commanded to distribute to others that which** is required **for** his **own** necessities and **those of his household ; nor even to give away what is** reasonably

---

*Timothy ii. 12.   † 2 Corinthians iv. 17.   ‡ St. Matthew **xix. 23, 24,**
§ St. Luke vi. 24, 25.   ‖ 2a 2æ Q. lxvi. Art. **2.**
¶ 2a 2æ Q. **lxv.** Art. **2.**

required to keep up becomingly his condition in life; *for no one ought to live unbecomingly.** But when necessity has been supplied, and one's position fairly considered, it is a duty to give to the indigent out of that which is over. *That which remaineth, give alms.*† It is a duty, not of justice (except in extreme cases), but of Christian charity—a duty which is not enforced by human law. But the laws and judgments of men must give place to the laws and judgments of Christ the true God, Who in many ways urges on his followers the practice of almsgiving—*It is more blessed to give than to receive;* ‡ and Who will count a kindness done or refused to the poor as done or refused to Himself—*as long as you did it to one of My least brethren, you did it to Me.* § Thus, to sum up what has been said: Whoever has received from the Divine bounty a large share of blessings, whether they be external and corporeal or gifts of the mind, has received them for the purpose of using them for the perfecting of his own nature, and, at the same time, that he may employ them, as the minister of God's Providence, for the benefit of others. *He that hath a talent*, says St. Gregory the Great, *let him see that he hide it not; he that hath abundance, let him arouse himself to mercy and generosity; he that hath art and skill, let him do his best to share the use and utility thereof with his neighbor.* ‖

25. As for those who do not possess the gifts of fortune, they are taught by the Church that, in God's sight poverty is no disgrace, and that there is nothing to be ashamed of in seeking one's bread by labor. This is strengthened by what we see in Christ Himself, Who *whereas He was rich, for our sakes became poor;* ¶ and Who, being the Son of God, and God Himself, chose to seem and to be considered the son of a carpenter—nay, did not disdain to spend a great part of His life as a carpenter Himself. *Is not this the carpenter, the Son of Mary?* ** From the contemplation of this Divine example it is easy to understand that the true dignity and excellence of man lies in his moral qualities, that is, in

---

* *Ibid.* Q. xxxii. Art. 6. † St. Luke xi. 41. ‡ Acts xx. 35.
§ St. Matthew xxv. 40. ‖ St. Gregory the Great, Hom. ix. *in Evangel.* n. 7.
¶ 2 Corinthians viii. 9. ** St. Mark vi. 3.

virtue; that virtue is the common inheritance of all, equally within the reach of high and low, rich and poor; and that virtue, and virtue alone, wherever found, will be followed by the rewards of everlasting happiness. Nay, God Himself seems to incline more to those who suffer evil; for Jesus Christ calls the poor blessed; * He lovingly invites those in labor and grief to come to Him for solace; † and He displays the tenderest charity to the lowly and the oppressed. These reflections cannot fail to keep down the pride of those who are well off, and to cheer the spirit of the afflicted; to incline the former to generosity and the latter to tranquil resignation. Thus the separation which pride would make tends to disappear, nor will it be difficult to make rich and poor join hands in friendly concord.

26. But, if Christian precepts prevail, the two classes will not only be united in the bonds of friendship but also in those of brotherly love. For they will understand and feel that all men are the children of the common Father, that is, of God; that all have the same last end, which is God Himself, Who alone can make either men or angels absolutely and perfectly happy; that all and each are redeemed by Jesus Christ and raised to the dignity of children of God, and are thus united in brotherly ties both with each other and with Jesus Christ, *the firstborn among many brethern;* that the blessings of nature and the gifts of grace belong in common to the whole human race, and that to all, except to those that are unworthy, is promised the inheritance of the Kingdom of Heaven. *If sons, heirs also; heirs indeed of God, and co-heirs of Christ.*‡

27. Such is the scheme of duties and of rights which is put forth to the world by the Gospel. Would it not seem that strife must quickly cease were society penetrated with ideas like these?

28. But the Church, not content with pointing out the remedy, also applies it. For the Church does its utmost to teach and to train men, and to educate them;

---

* St Matthew v. 3: "*Blessed are the poor in spirit.*"
† *Ibid.* xi. 28: "*Come to Me all you that labor and are burdened, and I will refresh you.*"
‡ Romans viii. 17.

and by means of its Bishops and Clergy it diffuses its salutary teachings far and wide. It strives to influence the mind and heart so that all may willingly yield themselves to be formed and guided by the commandments of God. It is precisely in this fundamental and principal matter, on which everything depends, that the Church has a power peculiar to itself. The agencies which it employs are given it for the very purpose of reaching the hearts of men, by Jesus Christ Himself, and derive their efficiency from God. They alone can touch the innermost heart and conscience, and bring men to act from a motive of duty, to resist their passions and appetites, to love God and their fellow-men with a love that is unique and supreme, and courageously to break down every barrier which stands in the way of a virtuous life.

29. On this subject We need only recall for one moment the examples written down in history. Of these things there cannot be the shadow of doubt; for instance, that civil society was renovated in every part by the teachings of Christianity; that in the strength of that renewal the human race was lifted up to better things—nay, that it was brought back from death to life, and to so excellent a life that nothing more perfect had been known before, or will come to pass in the ages that have yet to be. Of this beneficent transformation Jesus Christ was at once the first cause and the final purpose; as from Him all came, so to Him all was to be referred. For when, by the light of the Gospel message, the human race came to know the grand mystery of the Incarnation of the Word and the redemption of man, the life of Jesus Christ, God and Man, penetrated every race and nation, and impregnated them with His faith, His precepts, and His laws. And if Society is to be cured now, in no other way can it be cured but by a return to the Christian life and Christian institutions. When a society is perishing, the true advice to give to those who would restore it is, to recall it to the principles from which it sprung; for the purpose and perfection of an association is to aim at and to attain that for which it was formed; and its operation should be put in motion and inspired by the end and

object which originally gave it its being. So that to fall away from its primal constitution is disease; to go back to it is recovery. And this may be asserted with the utmost truth both of the State in general and of that body of its citizens—by far the greater number—who sustain life by labor.

20. Neither must it be supposed that the solicitude of the Church is so occupied with the spiritual concerns of its children as to neglect their interests temporal and earthly. Its desire is that the poor, for example, should rise above poverty and wretchedness, and should better their condition in life; and for this it strives. By the very fact that it calls men to virtue and forms them to its practice, it promotes this in no slight degree. Christian morality, when it is adequately and completely practiced, conduces of itself to temporal prosperity, for it merits the blessing of that God Who is the source of all blessings; it powerfully restrains the lust of possession and the lust of pleasure—twin plagues, which too often make a man without self-restraint miserable in the midst of abundance*; it makes men supply by economy for the want of means, teaching them to be content with frugal living, and keeping them out of the reach of those vices which eat up not merely small incomes, but large fortunes, and dissipate many a goodly inheritance.

31. Moreover, the Church intervenes directly in the interest of the poor, by setting on foot and keeping up many things which it sees to be efficacious in the relief of poverty. Here again it has always succeeded so well that it has even extorted the praise of its enemies. Such was the ardor of brotherly love among the earliest Christians that numbers of those who were better off deprived themselves of their possessions in order to relieve their brethren; whence *neither was there any one needy among them*†. To the order of Deacons, instituted for that very purpose, was committed by the Apostles the charge of the daily distributions; and the Apostle Paul, though burdened with the solicitude of

---

* "*The root of all evils is cupidity.*"—1 Tim. vi. 10.
† Acts iv. 34.

all the churches, hesitated not to undertake laborious journeys in order to carry the alms of the faithful to the poorer Christians. Tertullian calls these contributions, given voluntarily by Christians in their assemblies, *deposits of piety;* because, to cite his words, they were employed *in feeding the needy, in burying them, in the support of boys and girls destitute of means and deprived of their parents, in the care of the aged and in the relief of the shipwrecked.**

32. Thus by degrees came into existence the patrimony which the church has guarded with religious care as the inheritance of the poor. Nay, to spare them the shame of begging, the common Mother of rich and poor has exerted herself to gather together funds for the support of the needy. The Church has stirred up everywhere the heroism of charity, and has established Congregations of Religious and many other useful institutions for help and mercy, so that there might be hardly any kind of suffering which was not visited and relieved. At the present day there are many who, like the heathen of old, blame and condemn the Church for this beautiful charity. They would substitute in its place a system of State-organized relief. But no human methods will ever supply for the devotion and self-sacrifice of Christian charity. Charity, as a virtue, belongs to the Church; for it is no virtue unless it is drawn from the Sacred Heart of Jesus Christ; and he who turns his back on the Church cannot be near to Christ.

33. It cannot, however, be doubted that to attain the purpose of which We treat, not only the Church, but all human means must conspire. All who are concerned in the matter must be of one mind and must act together. It is in this, as in the Providence which governs the world; results do not happen save where all the causes coöperate.

34. Let us now, therefore, inquire what part the State should play in the work of remedy and relief.

35. By the State We here understand, not the particular form of government which prevails in this or that

---

* *Apologia Secunda,* xxxix.

nation, but the State as rightly understood; that is to say, any government conformable in its institutions to right reason and natural law, and to those dictates of the Divine wisdom which We have expounded in the Encyclical on the Christian Constitution of the State. The first duty, therefore, of the rulers of the S ate should be to make sure that the laws and institutions, the general character and administration of the commonwealth, shall be such as to produce of themselves public well-being and private prosperity. This is the proper office of wise statesmanship and the work of the heads of the State. Now, a State chiefly prospers and flourishes by morality, by well regulated family life, by respect for religion and justice, by the moderation and equal distribution of public burdens, by the progress of the arts and of trade, by the abundant yield of the land—by everything which makes the citizens better and happier. Here, then, it is in the power of a ruler to benefit every order of the State, and amongst the rest to promote in the highest degree the interests of the poor; and this by virtue of his office, and without being exposed to any suspicion of undue interference—for it is the province of the commonwealth to consult for the common good. And the more that is done for the working population by the general laws of the country, the less need will there be to seek for particular means to relieve them.

36. There is another and a deeper consideration which must not be lost sight of. To the State the interests of all are equal, whether high or low. The poor are members of the national community equally with the rich; they are real component parts, living parts, which make up, through the family, the living body; and it need hardly be said that they are by far the majority. It would be irrational to neglect one portion of the citizens and to favor another; and therefore the public administration must duly and solicitously provide for the welfare and the comfort of the working people, or else that law of justice will be violated which ordains that each shall have his due. To cite the wise words of St. Thomas of Aquin: *As the part and the whole are in a certain sense identical, the part*

may in some sense claim what belongs to the whole.* Among the many and grave duties of rulers who would do their best for the people, the first and chief is to act with strict justice—with that justice which is called in the Schools *distributive*—towards each and every class.

37. But although all citizens, without exception, can and ought to contribute to that common good in which individuals share so profitably to themselves, yet it is not to be supposed that all can contribute in the same way and to the same extent. No matter what changes may be made in forms of government, there will always be differences and inequalities of condition in the State: Society cannot exist or be conceived without them. Some there must be who dedicate themselves to the work of the commonwealth, who make the laws, who administer justice, whose advice and authority govern the nation in times of peace, and defend it in war. Such men clearly occupy the foremost place in the State, and should be held in the foremost estimation, for their work touches most nearly and effectively the general interests of the community. Those who labor at a trade or calling do not promote the general welfare in such a fashion as this; but they do in the most important way benefit the nation, though less directly. We have insisted that, since it is the end of society to make men better, the chief good that Society can be possessed of is Virtue. Nevertheless, in all well constituted States it is a by no means unimportant matter to provide those bodily and external commodities, *the use of which is necessary to virtuous action.*† And in the provision of material well being, the labor of the poor—the exercise of their skill and the employment of their strength in the culture of the land and the workshops of trade—is most efficacious and altogether indispensable. Indeed, their coöperation in this respect is so important that it may be truly said that it is only by the labor of the workingman that States grow rich. Justice, therefore, demands that the interests of the poorer population be carefully

---

* 2a 2æ Q. lxl. Art 1 ad 2.

† St. Thomas of Aquin. *De Regimine Principium*, I. cap. 15.

watched over by the Administration, so that they who contribute so largely to the advantage of the community may themselves share in the benefits they create—that being housed, clothed, and enabled to support life, they may find their existence less hard and more endurable. It follows that whatever shall appear to be conducive to the well being of those who work should receive favorable consideration. Let it not be feared that solicitude of this kind will injure any interest; on the contrary, it will be to the advantage of all; for it cannot but be good for the commonwealth to secure from misery those on whom it so largely depends.

38. We have said that the State must not absorb the individual or the family; both should be allowed free and untrammelled action as far as is consistent with the common good and the interest of others. Nevertheless, rulers should anxiously safeguard the community and all its parts; the community, because the conservation of the community is so emphatically the business of the supreme power that the safety of the commonwealth is not only the first law, but it is a Government's whole reason of existence; and the parts, because both philosophy and the gospel agree in laying down that the object of the administration of the State should be, not the advantage of the ruler but the benefit of those over whom he rules. The gift of authority is from God, and is, as it were, a participation of the highest of all sovereignties; and it should be exercised as the power of God is exercised—with a fatherly solicitude which not only guides the whole, but reaches to details as well.

39. Whenever the general interest of any particular class suffers, or is threatened with, evils which can in no other way be met, the public authority must step in to meet them. Now, among the interests of the public, as of private individuals, are these: that peace and good order should be maintained; that family life should be carried on in accordance with God's laws and those of nature; that religion should be reverenced and obeyed; that a high standard of morality should prevail in public and private life; that sanctity of justice should be respected, and that no one should injure another

with impunity; that the members of the commonwealth should grow up to man's estate strong and robust, and capable, if need be, of guarding and defending their country. If by a strike, or other combination of workmen, there should be imminent danger of disturbance to the public peace; or if circumstances were such that among the laboring population the ties of family life were relaxed; if Religion were found to suffer through the workmen not having time and opportunity to practice it; if in workshops and factories there were danger to morals through the mixing of the sexes or from any occasion of evil; or if employers laid burdens upon the workmen which were unjust, or degraded them with conditions that were repugnant to their dignity as human beings; finally, if health were endangered by excessive labor, or by work unsuited to sex or age—in these cases, there can be no question that, within certain limits, it would be right to call in the help and authority of the law. The limits must be determined by the nature of the occasion which calls for the law's interference—the principle being this, that the law must not undertake more, or go further, than is required for the remedy of the evil or the removal of the danger.

40. Rights must be religiously respected wherever they are found; and it is the duty of the public authority to prevent and punish injury, and to protect each one in the possession of his own. Still, when there is question of protecting the rights of individuals, the poor and helpless have a claim to special consideration. The richer population have many ways of protecting themselves, and stand less in need of help from the State; those who are badly off have no resources of their own to fall back upon, and must chiefly rely upon the assistance of the State. And it is for this reason that wage-earners, who are undoubtedly among the weak and necessitous, should be specially cared for and protected by the commonwealth.

41. Here, however, it will be advisable to advert expressly to one or two of the more important details. It must be borne in mind that the chief thing to be secured is the safeguarding, by legal enactment and

policy, of private property. Most of all is it essential in these times of covetous greed, to keep the multitude within the line of duty; for if all may justly strive to better their condition, yet neither justice nor the common good allows any one to seize that which belongs to another, or, under the pretext of futile and ridiculous equality, to lay hands on other people's fortunes. It is most true that by far the larger part of the people who work prefer to improve themselves by honest labor rather than by doing wrong to others. But there are not a few who are imbued with bad principles and are anxious for revolutionary change, and whose great purpose it is to stir up tumult and bring about a policy of violence. The authority of the State should intervene to put restraint upon these disturbers, to save the workmen from their seditious arts, and to protect lawful owners from spoliation.

42. When work people have recourse to a strike, it is frequently because the hours of labor are too long, or the work too hard, or because they consider their wages insufficient. The grave inconvenience of this not uncommon occurrence should be obviated by public remedial measures; for such paralysis of labor not only affects the masters and their work people, but is extremely injurious to trade, and to the general interests of the public; moreover, on such occasions, violence and disorder are generally not far off, and thus it frequently happens that the public peace is threatened. The laws should be beforehand, and prevent these troubles from arising; they should lend their influence and authority to the removal in good time of the causes which lead to conflicts between masters and those whom they employ.

43. But if the owners of property must be made secure, the Workman, too, has property and possessions in which he must be protected; and, first of all, there are his spiritual and mental interests. Life on earth, however good and desirable in itself, is not the final purpose for which man is created; it is only the way and the means to that attainment of truth, and that practice of goodness in which the full life of the soul consists. It is the soul which is made after the image and likeness of God; it is in the soul that sovereignty

resides, in virtue of which man is commanded to rule the creatures below him, and to use all the earth and the ocean for his profit and advantage. *Fill the earth and subdue it; and rule over the fishes of the sea, and the fowls of the air, and all living creatures which move upon the earth.** In this respect all men are equal; there is no difference between rich and poor, master and servant, ruler and ruled, *for the same is lord over all.*† No man may outrage with impunity that human dignity which God Himself treats *with reverence,* nor stand in the way of that higher life which is the preparation for the eternal life of Heaven. Nay, more; a man has here no power over himself. To consent to any treatment which is calculated to defeat the end and purpose of his being is beyond his right; he cannot give up his soul to servitude; for it is not man's own rights which are here in question, but the rights of God, most sacred and inviolable.

44. From this follows the obligation of the cessation of work and labor on Sundays and certain festivals. This rest from labor is not to be understood as mere idleness; much less must it be an occasion of spending money and of vicious excess, as many would desire it to be; but it should be rest from labor consecrated by religion. Repose united with religious observance disposes man to forget for a while the business of this daily life, and to turn his thoughts to heavenly things and to the worship which he so strictly owes to the Eternal Deity. It is this, above all, which is the reason and motive of the Sunday rest; a rest sanctioned by God's great law of the ancient covenant, *Remember thou keep holy the Sabbath Day,*‡ and taught to the world by His own mysterious "rest" after the creation of man; *He rested on the seventh day from all His work which He had done.*§

45. If we turn now to things exterior and corporeal, the first concern of all is to save the poor workers from the cruelty of grasping speculators, who use human beings as mere instruments for making money. It is neither justice nor humanity so to grind men down

---

* Genesis i. 28.   † Romans x. 12.   ‡ Exod. xx. 8.   § Genesis ii. 2.

with excessive labor as to stupefy their minds and wear out their bodies. Man's powers, like his general nature, are limited, and beyond these limits he cannot go. His strength is developed and increased by use and exercise, but only on condition of due intermission and proper rest. Daily labor, therefore, must be so regulated that it may not be protracted during longer hours than strength admits. How many and how long the intervals of rest should be, will depend on the nature of the work, on circumstances of time and place, and on the health and strength of the workman. Those who labor in mines and quarries, and in work within the bowels of the earth, should have shorter hours in proportion as their labor is more severe and more trying to health. Then, again, the season of the year must be taken into account; for not unfrequently a kind of labor is easy at one time which at another is intolerable or very difficult. Finally, work which is suitable for a strong man cannot reasonably be required from a woman or a child. And, in regard to children, great care should be taken not to place them in workshops and factories until their bodies and minds are sufficiently mature. For just as rough weather destroys the buds of Spring, so too early an experience of life's hard work blights the young promise of a child's powers, and makes any real education impossible. Women, again, are not suited to certain trades; for a woman is by nature fitted for home work, and, it is that which is best adapted at once to preserve her modesty and to promote the good bringing up of children and the well being of the family. As a general principle it may be laid down that a workman ought to have leisure and rest in proportion to the wear and tear of his strength; for the waste of strength must be repaired by the cessation of work.

46. In all agreements between masters and work people there is always the condition, expressed or understood, that there be allowed proper rest for soul and body. To agree in any other sense would be against what is right and just; for it can never be right or just to require on the one side, or to promise on the other,

the giving **up of those** duties which a man owes to his God and to himself.

47. We now **approach a subject of** very great importance, **and one on which, if extremes** are to be avoided, **right ideas are absolutely necessary.** Wages, we are told, **are fixed by free consent; and,** therefore, the employer, **when he pays what was agreed upon,** has done **his part and is not called upon for anything** further. **The only way, it is said, in which injustice could** happen **would be if the master refused to pay the whole of** the wages, or the workman **would not** complete **the work** undertaken; **when** this happens the State **should intervene, to see** that each obtains his own—**but not under any other circumstances.**

48. **This mode of reasoning is by** no means convincing to a fair-minded **man, for there are** important considerations **which it leaves out of view altogether.** To labor is **to exert one's self for the sake of** procuring **what is necessary for the** purposes **of life, and most** of all for **self-preservation.** *In the sweat of thy brow thou shall eat bread.** Therefore a man's labor has **two notes or characters. First of all, it is** *personal,* **for the exertion of individual power** belongs to the individual who **puts it forth, employing this** power for that personal **profit for which it was given.** Secondly, man's labor is *necessary,* **for without the results** of labor a man cannot live; **and self-conservation is a** law of Nature, **which it is wrong to disobey. Now,** if we were to consider labor **merely so far as it is** *personal,* doubtless it would be **within the workman's right to accept any rate of wages whatever; for in the same way as he is free to work or not, so he is free to accept** a small remuneration **or even none** at all. **But this is a mere abstract** supposition; **the** labor **of the workingman is not only his** personal attribute, **but it is** *necessary;* **and** this makes **all the** difference. The preservation **of** life is the bounden **duty of each and** all, and to fail **therein is** a crime. **It follows that each one has** a right to procure what is required **in order to** live, and the **poor** can procure it **in no** other way than by work and wages.

---

* Genesis iii. 19.

49. Let it be granted then that, as a rule, workman and employer should make free agreements, and in particular should freely agree as to wages; nevertheless, there is a dictate of nature more imperious and more ancient than any bargain between man and man, that the remuneration must be enough to support the wage-earner in reasonable and frugal comfort. If through necessity or fear of a worse evil the workman accepts harder conditions because an employer or a contractor will give him no better, he is the victim of force and injustice. In these and similar questions, however—such as, for example, the hours of labor in different trades, the sanitary precautions to be observed in factories and workshops, etc.—in order to supersede undue interference on the part of the State, especially as circumstances, times, and localities differ so widely, it is advisable that recourse be had to Societies or Boards such as We shall mention presently, or to some other method of safeguarding the interests of wage earners; the State to be asked for approval and protection.

50. If a workman's wages be sufficient to enable him to maintain himself, his wife, and his children in reasonable comfort, he will not find it difficult, if he is a sensible man, to study economy; and he will not fail, by cutting down expenses, to put by a little property; nature and reason would urge him to this. We have seen that this great Labor question cannot be solved except by assuming as a principle that private ownership must be held sacred and inviolable. The law, therefore, should favor ownership, and its policy should be to induce as many of the people as possible to become owners.

51. Many excellent results will follow from this; and first of all, property will certainly become more equitably divided. For the effect of civil change and revolution has been to divide society into two widely differing castes. On the one side, there is the party which holds the power because it holds the wealth; which has in its grasp all labor and all trade, which manipulates for its own benefit and its own purposes all the sources of supply, and which is powerfully rep-

resented in the councils of the State itself. On the other side there is the needy and powerless multitude, sore and suffering, and always ready for disturbance. If working people can be encouraged to look forward to obtaining a share in the land, the result will be that the gulf between vast wealth and deep poverty will be bridged over, and the two orders will be brought nearer together. Another consequence will be the greater abundance of the fruits of the earth. Men always work harder and more readily when they work on that which is their own; nay, they learn to love the very soil which yields in response to the labor of their hands, not only food to eat, but an abundance of good things for themselves and those that are dear to them. It is evident how such a spirit of willing labor would add to the produce of the earth and to the wealth of the community. And a third advantage would arise from this: men would cling to the country in which they were born; for no one would exchange his country for a foreign land if his own afforded him the means of living a tolerable and happy life. These three important benefits, however, can only be expected on the condition that a man's means be not drained and exhausted by excessive taxation. The right to possess private property is from nature, not from man; and the State has only the right to regulate its use in the interests of the public good, but by no means to abolish it altogether. The State is therefore unjust and cruel if, in the name of taxation, it deprives the private owner of more than is just.

52. In the last place—employers and workmen may themselves effect much in the matter of which We treat, by means of those institutions and organizations which afford opportune assistance to those in need, and which draw the two orders more closely together. Among these may be enumerated: Societies for mutual help; various foundations established by private persons for providing for the workman, and for his widow or his orphans, in sudden calamity, in sickness, and in the event of death; and what are called "patronages" or institutions for the care of boys and girls, for young people and also for those of more mature age.

53. The most important of all are **Workmen's Associations**; for these virtually include all the rest. History attests what excellent results were effected by the Artificers' Guilds of a former day. They were the means not only of many advantages to the workmen, but in no small degree of the advancement of art, as numerous monuments remain to **prove.** Such associations should be adapted to the **requirements of** the age in which we live—an age of greater **instruction,** of different customs, and of more numerous **requirements in daily life. It is** gratifying to know **that there are actually in existence not a few** Societies **of this nature,** consisting **either of workmen** alone or of workmen and **employers** together; but it **were greatly to be** desired that they should multiply and **become more** effective. We have spoken of them more than **once; but it will be** well to explain here how **much they are needed, to** show that they **exist** by **their own right, and to** enter into their **organization and their work.**

54. The experience of his own weakness urges man to call in help from without. We read in the pages of Holy Writ: *It is better that two should be together than* one *; for they have the advantage of their society. If* one *fall he shall be supported by the other. Woe to him that is alone, for when he falleth he hath none to lift him up.** And further: *A brother that is helped by his brother is like a strong city.*† It is this natural impulse which unites men in civil society; and it is this also which makes them band themselves together in associations of citizen with **citizen**; **associations which, it is true, cannot be called** societies **in the complete sense of the word, but which** are societies **nevertheless.**

55. These lesser societies and **the** society which constitutes the State differ in many things, because their **immediate** purpose and end is different. Civil **society exists for** the common good, and **therefore is concerned with the interests** of all **in general, and with individual interests in their** due place and proportion. Hence it is called *public* society, because by its means, as St. Thomas of Aquin says, *Men communicate with one an-*

---

* Ecclesiastes iv. 9, 10.   † Proverbs xviii. **19.**

other in the setting up of a commonwealth.* But the societies which are formed in the bosom of the State are called *private*, and justly so, because their immediate purpose is the private advantage of the associates. *Now a private society*, says St. Thomas again, *is one which is formed for the purpose of carrying out private business ; as when two or three enter into a partnership with the view of trading in conjunction.*† Particular societies, then, although they exist within the State, and are each a part of the State, nevertheless cannot be prohibited by the State absolutely and as such. For to enter into "society" of this kind is the natural right of man; and the State must protect natural rights, not destroy them ; and if it forbids its citizens to form associations, it contradicts the very principle of its own existence ; for both they and it exist in virtue of the same principle, viz., the natural propensity of man to live in society.

56. There are times, no doubt, when it is right that the law should interfere to prevent association; as when men join together for purposes which are evidently bad, unjust, or dangerous to the State. In such cases the public authority may justly forbid the formation of associations, and may dissolve them when they already exist. But every precaution should be taken not to violate the rights of individuals and not to make unreasonable regulations under the pretense of public benefit. For laws only bind when they are in accordance with right reason, and therefore with the eternal law of God.‡

57. And here we are reminded of the Confraternities, Societies, and Religious Orders, which have arisen by the Church's authority and the piety of the Christian people. The annals of every nation down to our own times testify to what they have done for the human race. It is indisputable, on grounds of reason alone, that such associations, being perfectly blameless in their objects, have the

---

* *Contra impugnantes Dei cultum et religionem*, Cap. II.   † *Ibid.*

‡ *Human law is law only in virtue of its accordance with right reason ; and thus it is manifest that it flows from the eternal law. And in so far as it deviates from right reason it is called an unjust law ; in such case it is not law at all, but rather a species of violence.*—St. Thomas of Aquin, *Summa Theologica*, 1a 2æ Q. xciii. Art. III.

sanction of the law of nature. On their religious side they rightly claim to be responsible to the Church alone. The administrators of the State, therefore, have no rights over them, nor can they claim any share in their management; on the contrary, it is the State's duty to respect and cherish them, and, if necessary, to defend them from attack. It is notorious that a very different course has been followed, more especially in our own times. In many places the State has laid violent hands on these communities, and committed manifold injustice against them; it has placed them under the civil law, taken away their rights as corporate bodies, and robbed them of their property. In such property the Church had her rights, each member of the body had his or her rights, and there were also the rights of those who had founded or endowed them for a definite purpose, and of those for whose benefit and assistance they existed. Wherefore We cannot refrain from complaining of such spoliation as unjust and fraught with evil results; and with the more reason because, at the very time when the law proclaims that association is free to all, We see that Catholic societies, however peaceable and useful, are hindered in every way, whilst the utmost freedom is given to men whose objects are at once hurtful to Religion and dangerous to the State.

58. Associations of every kind, and especially those of workingmen, are now far more common than formerly. In regard to many of these there is no need at present to inquire whence they spring, what are their objects, or what means they use. But there is a good deal of evidence which goes to prove that many of these societies are in the hands of invisible leaders, and are managed on principles far from compatible with Christianity and the public well being; and that they do their best to get into their hands the whole field of labor and to force workmen either to join them or to starve. Under these circumstances Christian workmen must do one of two things: either join Associations in which their religion will be exposed to peril, or form associations among themselves—unite their forces and courageously shake off the yoke of an unjust and intolerable oppression. No one who does not wish to

expose man's chief good to extreme danger will hesitate to say that the second alternative must by all means be adopted.

59. Those Catholics are worthy of all praise—and there are not a few—who, understanding what the times require, have, by various enterprises and experiments, endeavored to better the condition of the working people without any sacrifice of principle. They have taken up the cause of the workingman, and have striven to make both families and individuals better off; to infuse the spirit of justice into the mutual relations of employer and employed; to keep before the eyes of both classes the precepts of duty and the laws of the Gospel—that Gospel which, by inculcating self-restraint, keeps men within the bounds of moderation, and tends to establish harmony among the divergent interests and various classes which compose the State. It is with such ends in view that We see men of eminence meeting together for discussion, for the promotion of united action, and for practical work. Others, again, strive to unite working people of various kinds into associations, help them with their advice and their means, and enable them to obtain honest and profitable work. The Bishops, on their part, bestow their ready good will and support; and with their approval and guidance many members of the clergy, both secular and regular, labor assiduously on behalf of the spiritual and mental interests of the members of Associations. And there are not wanting Catholics possessed of affluence who have, as it were, cast in their lot with the wage-earners, and who have spent large sums in founding and widely spreading Benefit and Insurance Societies; by means of which the workingman may without difficulty acquire by his labor not only many present advantages, but also the certainty of honorable support in time to come. How much this multiplied and earnest activity has benefited the community at large is too well known to require Us to dwell upon it. We find in it the grounds of the most cheering hope for the future; provided that the Associations We have described continue to grow and spread, and are well and wisely administered. Let the State watch over

these Societies of citizens united together in the exercise of their right ; but let it not thrust itself into their peculiar concerns and their organization ; for things move and live by the soul within them, and they may be killed by the grasp of a hand from without.

60. In order that an Association may be carried on with unity of purpose and harmony of action, its organization and government must be firm and wise. All such Societies, being free to exist, have the further right to adopt such rules and organization as may best conduce to the attainment of their objects. We do not deem it possible to enter into definite details on the subject of organization : this must depend on national character, on practice and experience, on the nature and scope of the work to be done, on the magnitude of the various trades and employments, and on other circumstances of fact and of time—all of which must be carefully weighed.

61. Speaking summarily, we may lay it down as a general and perpetual law, that Workmen's Associations should be so organized and governed as to furnish the best and most suitable means for attaining what is aimed at, that is to say, for helping each individual member to better his condition to the utmost in body, mind, and property. It is clear that they must pay special and principal attention to piety and morality, and that their internal discipline must be directed precisely by these considerations ; otherwise they entirely lose their special character, and come to be very little better than those Societies which take no account of Religion at all. What advantage can it be to a Workman to obtain by means of a Society all that he requires, and to endanger his soul for want of spiritual food? *What doth it profit a man if he gain the whole world and suffer the loss of his own soul?* * This, as Our Lord teaches, is the note or character that distinguishes the Christian from the heathen. *After all these things do the heathens seek. . . . Seek ye first the Kingdom of God and His justice, and all these things shall be added unto you.*† Let our associations,

---

* St. Matthew xvi. 26. † St. Matthew vi. 32, 33.

then, look first and before all to God; let religious instruction have therein a foremost place, each one being carefully taught what is his duty to God, what to believe, what to hope for, and how to work out his salvation; and let all be warned and fortified with especial solicitude against wrong opinions and false teaching. Let the workingman be urged and led to the worship of God, to the earnest practice of religion, and, among other things, to the sanctification of Sundays and festivals. Let him learn to reverence and love Holy Church, the common Mother of us all; and so to obey the precepts and to frequent the Sacraments of the Church, those Sacraments being the means ordained by God for obtaining forgiveness of sin and for leading a holy life.

62. The foundations of the organization being laid in Religion, we next go on to determine the relations of the members one to another, in order that they may live together in concord and go on prosperously and successfully. The offices and charges of the Society should be distributed for the good of the Society itself, and in such manner that difference in degree or position should not interfere with unanimity and goodwill. Office bearers should be appointed with prudence and discretion, and each one's charge should be carefully marked out; thus no member will suffer wrong. Let the common funds be administered with the strictest honesty, in such way that a member receive assistance in proportion to his necessities. The rights and duties of employers should be the subject of careful consideration as compared with the rights and duties of the employed. If it should happen that either a master or a workman deemed himself injured, nothing would be more desirable than that there should be a committee composed of honest and capable men of the Association itself, whose duty it should be, by the laws of the Association, to decide the dispute. Among the purposes of a Society should be to try to arrange for a continuous supply of work at all times and seasons; and to create a fund from which the members may be helped in their necessities, not only in cases of accident, but also in sickness, old age, and misfortune.

63. Such rules and regulations, if obeyed willingly by all, will sufficiently insure the well-being of poor people; whilst such mutual Associations among Catholics are certain to be productive, in no small degree, of prosperity to the State. It is not rash to conjecture the future from the past. Age gives way to age, but the events of one century are wonderfully like those of another; for they are directed by the Providence of God, who overrules the course of history in accordance with His purposes in creating the race of man. We are told that it was cast as a reproach on the Christians of the early ages of the Church, that the greater number of them had to live by begging or by labor. Yet, destitute as they were of wealth and influence, they ended by winning over to their side the favor of the rich and the good will of the powerful. They showed themselves industrious, laborious, and peaceful, men of justice, and, above all, men of brotherly love. In the presence of such a life and such an example prejudice disappeared, the tongue of malevolence was silenced, and the lying traditions of ancient superstition yielded little by little to Christian truth.

64. At this moment the condition of the working population is the question of the hour; and nothing can be of higher interest to all classes of the State than that it should be rightly and reasonably decided. But it will be easy for Christian workingmen to decide it right if they form Associations, choose wise guides, and follow the same path which with so much advantage to themselves and the commonwealth was trod by their fathers before them. Prejudice, it is true, is mighty, and so is the love of money; but if the sense of what is just and right be not destroyed by depravity of heart, their fellow citizens are sure to be won over to a kindly feeling towards men whom they see to be so industrious and so modest, who so unmistakably prefer honesty to lucre, and the sacredness of duty to all other considerations.

65. And another great advantage would result from the state of things We are describing: there would be so much more hope and possibility of recalling to a sense of their duty those workingmen who have either

given up their faith altogether, or whose lives are at variance with its precepts. These men, in most cases, feel that they have been fooled by empty promises and deceived by false appearances. They cannot but perceive that their grasping employers too often treat them with the greatest inhumanity and hardly care for them beyond the profit their labor brings; and if they belong to an Association, it is probably one in which there exists, in place of charity and love, that intestine strife which always accompanies unresigned and irreligious poverty. Broken in spirit and worn down in body, how many of them would gladly free themselves from this galling slavery! But human respect, or the dread of starvation, makes them afraid to take the step. To such as these Catholic Associations are of incalculable service, helping them out of their difficulties, inviting them to companionship, and receiving the repentant to a shelter in which they may securely trust.

66. We have now laid before you, Venerable Brethren, who are the persons and what are the means, by which this most difficult question must be solved. Every one must put his hand to the work which falls to his share, and that at once and immediately, lest the evil which is already so great may by delay become absolutely beyond remedy. Those who rule the State must use the law and the institutions of the country; masters and rich men must remember their duty; the poor whose interests are at stake, must make every lawful and proper effort; and since Religion alone, as We said at the beginning, can destroy the evil at its root, all men must be persuaded that the primary thing needful is to return to real Christianity, in the absence of which all the plans and devices of the wisest will be of little avail.

67. As far as regards the Church, its assistance will never be wanting, be the time or the occasion what it may; and it will intervene with the greater effect in proportion as its liberty of action is the more unfettered: let this be carefully noted by those whose office it is to provide for the public welfare. Every minister of holy Religion must throw into the conflict all the energy of his mind and all the strength of his endu-

rance; with your authority Venerable Brethren, and by your example, they must never cease to urge upon all men of every class, upon the high as well as the lowly, the Gospel doctrines of Christian life; by every means in their power they must strive for the good of the people; and above all they must earnestly cherish in themselves, and try to arouse in others, Charity, the mistress and queen of virtues. For the happy results we all long for must be chiefly brought about by the plenteous outpouring of Charity; of that true Christian Charity which is the fulfilling of the whole Gospel law, which is always ready to sacrifice itself for others' sake, and which is man's surest antidote against worldly pride and immoderate love of self; that Charity whose office is described and whose Godlike features are drawn by the Apostle St. Paul in these words: *Charity is patient, is kind . . . seeketh not her own . . . suffereth all things . . . endureth all things.**

68. On each one of you, Venerable Brethren, and on your Clergy and people, as an earnest of God's mercy and a mark of our affection, We lovingly in the Lord bestow the Apostolic Benediction.

Given at St. Peter's, in Rome, the fifteenth day of May, 1891, the fourteenth year of Our Pontificate.

LEO XIII., POPE.

---

* I Corinthians xiii. 4-7.

www.ingramcontent.com/pod-product-compliance
Lightning Source LLC
Chambersburg PA
CBHW030312170426
43202CB00009B/978